Enjoy the journey,

MW01164739

KNOWING
WHO
YOU LEAD

Important lessons on why we need to understand those we lead

By Carrie-Lynn Hotson

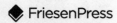 FriesenPress

One Printers Way
Altona, MB R0G 0B0
Canada

www.friesenpress.com

For information on discounts and bulk pricing options, please contact the author at www.inspiringorganizationalgrowth.ca

Knowing Who You Lead is a work of non-fiction. Nonetheless, some of the names and characteristics of the individuals involved have been changed in order to disguise their identities. Any resulting resemblance to persons living or dead is entirely coincidental and unintentional.

ISBN
978-1-03-914231-2 (Hardcover)
978-1-03-914230-5 (Paperback)
978-1-03-914232-9 (eBook)

1. BUSINESS & ECONOMICS, HUMAN RESOURCES & PERSONNEL MANAGEMENT

Distributed to the trade by The Ingram Book Company

Book Testimonials

It has been said that the most important rule in public speaking is knowing your audience. In her new book, Carrie-Lynn Hotson successfully extends this thinking to leadership, that is, the importance of knowing the people you lead. She does so in a very practical way with real-life examples that drive home her key points. The book will be a valuable resource for people who are either new to leadership or who are quite experienced. In particular, its value will be recognized in organizations who foster the personal growth and wellbeing of all their human resources.

Dr. Michel Lariviere, C.Psych
Clinical psychologist and Professor

In Knowing Who You Lead, Carrie-Lynn Hotson combines her extensive Human Resources experience with powerful people analytics to diagnose common workplace people challenges and provides Human Resources leaders with strategies to overcome these obstacles.

Mitch LePage,
Superintendent of Education (Retired)

Hotson takes us beyond the courses, training and knowledge and skills we already have and provides us with new leadership lessons while she illustrates how to combine and utilize these new skills to improve our approaches and success as a leader. She poignantly describes the importance of learning about the people we lead and getting to know what makes them tick, how they learn, who they are, what drives them, what triggers them and how they address conflict. Further, she graphically illustrates how this valuable information can assist leaders in effectively addressing employees through all their stages of employment.

Allan R. Lekun
Deputy Police Chief (Retired)

As a former university professor and veteran human resources practitioner, I believe that both novice and experts in the leadership field could equally and greatly benefit from reading this book. Carrie-Lynn has cleverly fashioned a book that provides some very practical scenarios and examples, along with critical-thinking questions that encourages the reader to undertake some self-reflection as to how they would lead in various situations. I would recommend this book to anyone who is looking at honing their leadership style for the successful mentoring and coaching any type of team in many different realms. The application of the concepts herein provides the reader with the tools to succeed in the workplace, with a sport team, an association, or even within family.

Marcel Faggioni
President, Integrity Management
Consulting Group

Dedication

This book is dedicated to my family and friends who *believed* in me, who gave me the *courage* to be both vulnerable and honest in my writing, and who *trusted* me to share their stories and experiences with you, the reader.

Table of Contents

PART 1 — IT ALL STARTS WITH YOU

LESSON 1

We Can't Do It Alone

LESSON 2

We Are Missing the Key Link

PART 2 — WHO ARE YOU LEADING?

LESSON 8
Rely on Data

PART 3 — DEVELOPING TRUST, REMOVING TRIGGERS, AND BUILDING TEAMS

LESSON 9
A One-Size-Fits-All Approach Doesn't Work

LESSON 10
Learning How You Impact Others

PART 4 — PUTTING LESSONS LEARNED INTO PRACTICE

PART 5 — INSPIRING ORGANIZATIONAL GROWTH

INTRODUCTION—ASKING WHY

I have always been someone who asks *"why?"* My mind is always thinking of ways to potentially improve things, question things, and trying to understand what is behind the issue at hand. When it comes to leadership and coaching people on how to reach their greatest potential, of course I have to ask, *"why doesn't it always work out the way we planned?"*

Exploring *Why*

- *Why* as leaders do we always seem to be chasing the next best leadership strategy and course but still struggle with the same challenges?
- *Why* do people who joined an organization enthused and excited become disgruntled and negative only a few years later?
- *Why* are some leaders revered, while others are not? What is the difference?
- *Why* do some people not seem to reach their fullest potential?
- *Why* do workplace issues and conflict remain so difficult to resolve?

Willingness to be Vulnerable

Every role I have filled—trainee, coach, supervisor, manager, parent, and mediator—has required me to be vulnerable in order to learn. This lesson has assisted me in my journey of examining these questions and developing some innovative strategies leaders can try. I have been the trainee who came into the workplace only understanding the theory behind the work but needing to be exposed to real-world issues. In reality, I didn't know what I didn't know! When I think back to my experiences with one of my workplace coaches, my memories are mired with both laughter and frustration. We came from two very different times. He had a command-and-control type of leadership. I will never forget Ray telling me *"Forget everything they taught you in school. I am going to teach you how it really is."* When I inevitably asked too many questions and wanted to challenge the status quo on *why* things were done the way they were, he put me on a *question timeout* to give himself a break! We fought, we argued, we laughed, and we became the best of friends. *"Why?"* you may ask. Because along the way, we took the time to learn what made each of us tick, who we were as people, what our strengths were, and when we felt most vulnerable. We got to know each other as people, and we learned to value and respect each other's strengths and talents. We didn't try to change the other person; we learned to appreciate them. Ironically, years later, Ray is now retired and teaches at a local college. Who does he call on to mentor his class in learning to develop their resume, prepare for interviews, and highlight their own strengths? Me! We have great sessions with the students, sharing stories of those dreaded first coaching sessions, and inspiring them to develop a very good understanding of who they are as people and potential employees.

Years later, after working with Ray, I too would become the coach. I was so excited to try and help the next generation learn the ins and outs of the job and develop the needed skills and experience to succeed. I remember reading all the leadership books and coaching habits I could find. I was convinced I would be a great coach. Some of the experiences went well, and we too created lasting relationships. Sadly, however, some of my trainees may feel a little differently about how successful their experience was. They may look back on the experience as being frustrating and uninspiring. They still became great employees, very skilled and professional. So why did the coaching experience seem flat and involve two people who were constantly butting heads? What was I missing? Did our failed initial relationship then impact the trust and respect we had for each other throughout the rest of our professional relationship? What could I have done differently?

Answering the *Why*

To answer this question, I have also thought about the relationships I have developed with other colleagues, workmates, and supervisors over the last 25 years. Which ones did I treasure the most? Which ones were the most challenging? Which ones did I want to emulate? And *why*?

Over the years, I have worked very hard to examine these exact questions. I have taken more leadership training, studied to be a human resources professional, trained to become a mediator and an interview coach, and risen through the ranks of supervision and leadership to that of a senior manager. I push myself to try and better understand *why* some professional relationships seem to develop into a genuine sense of trust and respect where trainees feel safe to learn, ask questions, and grow together, while in others they remain guarded and feel unsupported. What impact does this have on the individuals, the work they are both doing together, and inevitably the organization they work for?

As the facilitator of many leadership and coach development training sessions, I like to challenge my participants to examine these questions and concepts with me.

- *Why* are some people easier to lead than others?
- *What* do you admire in an effective leader and *why*?
- *Why* do some of your leadership strategies not work with certain people?
- *What* do you wish your leader knew about you and *why*?

Leadership Development Stages—The Five Parts

As I began to teach and work with coaches, leaders, and supervisors, I realized that in order to become effective, we need to take our leadership development in stages. Regardless of whether you are just starting out in your leadership journey or have decades of experience, there is always more to learn and examine. Therefore, this book is broken up into five parts, moving from who you are, to who you lead, to developing trust and building teams, to putting lessons into practice, and finally to how we can truly effect organizational change.

Part 1—It All Starts with You

a. First, we need to challenge who we are—examine our own values, behaviours, strengths, and preferences. There are so many fantastic books, seminars, podcasts, and TED Talks that teach us how to do exactly that. I will highlight many in this book, explaining what I have taken from each of them, and the lessons and practices that I have tried to incorporate in my own leadership journey.

b. Next, we need to expand these ideas into a new set of *whys*. This is where real growth and learning can occur. So many of us, myself included, have walked away from leadership courses and training with a better understanding of who we are, armed with a variety of leadership strategies we can utilize. We put a genuine effort into self-improvement and trying to inspire organizational change. But for some reason, it doesn't work. *Why? What are we missing?*

Part 2—Who Are You Leading?

c. A key portion of our learning will also involve getting to *know* our employees, learning about their traits, needs, interests, learning styles, and behaviours. This will play a key role in helping us to effectively lead and inspire them.

d. Learning how to address the underlying issues is also pivotal to retaining employees. My years in human resources, facilitation, interview coaching, and helping people deal with conflicts helped to enlighten me into why people stay, and why others don't. This time, the trainees, the employees, and the disgruntled members who were leaving organizations became my teachers. Through them I started to uncover what it was we as leaders were missing, how we may be failing them and causing our organizations to remain stuck and subject to low morale and grievances. Over and over people spoke of the need to feel appreciated, valued, and respected. In his speech on coaching millennials, Ken Hitchcock famously said, "Boost hearts and you will boost minds."[1] By learning how to do this, we can ultimately improve the bottom line in production and efficiency costs, retention, grievances, and succession planning. Happy employees stay with their leaders. They want to work for you.

Part 3—Developing Trust, Removing Triggers, and Building Teams

e. Sometimes we fail to take into consideration how vulnerable we as leaders need to be to earn the trust of our employees. Trust is linked to many core values of honesty, respect, loyalty, commitment, and integrity. These qualities are the very ones that my survey participants listed as imperative when answering questions focused on "what makes an effective supervisor."

f. To build effective teams, we will need to use identified strategies to help them get to know each other, identify their strengths and how they interact with each other. You will need to learn what triggers them, how they want to learn, and what they need to be successful.

Part 4—Putting Lessons Learned into Practice

g. It's the era of virtual leadership. An emerging virtual workforce has created the need for leaders to learn how to engage with employees they rarely, if ever, meet in person. The use of social media platforms, virtual meetings, and written communication presents new challenges. Leaders will need to adjust their own behaviours and styles to ensure their remote employees feel engaged, included, and willing to remain loyal to their organizations.

h. Dealing with conflict is inevitable. However, if we focus only on the incident, talking to witnesses, proving the "case," finding fault, it does absolutely *nothing* to resolve the underlying issues. Years later, the same employees still foster distrust for each other and the organization. They still can't work together, and now you have to take great efforts to ensure their comfort by placing them in different

---

1   Ken Hitchcock's speech on "About Coaching Millennials" can be found on Coach Kirill's YouTube Channel https://youtu.be/lmsvDHeXWmE

work groups, under different supervision, and even ensure they don't have to attend training sessions together. It can be exhausting for leaders and soul crushing for those involved. We need to learn to get to the root of the issue.

i.   We will apply these lessons to dealing with conflict, performance management, and helping your staff reach whatever goals have been have set. We will examine the need to listen, and how to do it effectively so that we can determine the underlying issues and concerns the speaker has. Only then can we determine what employees really need from us.

Part 5—Inspiring Organizational Growth

j.   Finally, we will move to a focus on equity, diversity, and inclusion with respect to bringing new ideas, new backgrounds, and new experiences into your workforce. We will explore what that means to you and to your organization. We will discuss some of the challenging definitions and examine why everyone does not hold the same meaning to these words. Diversity and inclusion work requires all of us to be vulnerable, openly demonstrate a willingness to work with people different than ourselves, recognize our own biases, and develop an appreciation for the way in which differences make us all unique and special.

k.   We will discuss the need for organizations to expand their definitions of diversity and how they will approach hiring and retention and ensuring that they are being inclusive. Additionally, we will examine the risk of labels and assumptions. Much of this work will start with learning *how* the diversity a person brings from their lived experience can potentially enhance your organization, and what you need to do to ensure they feel *respected and valued*.

20 Lessons I Have Learned

I will provide you with 20 lessons I have learned, mistakes I have made, real tools you can utilize, and strategies you can implement to get to know both yourself and those you lead better. I hope as we go along, you will also think of your own examples and experiences and have a willingness to ask:

- What can you learn from others about yourself and how you lead?
- What do you need know about the people you lead?
- Are your own assumptions and preferences impacting your team?
- How can you truly inspire others?
- What does it mean to be truly inclusive?

PART 1

—

IT ALL STARTS
WITH YOU

LESSON 1

We Can't Do It Alone
How We Learn to Play Hockey

Ineed to warn you that this book is not for the faint of heart. Before you read it, be honest with yourself. Do you tend to pick up a leadership book, flip through the lessons, think *I know this already*, and then close the book without really doing a deep dive into what it is telling you about yourself, your tendencies, your habits? The intent of this book is to challenge you, to get you to think about many of the concepts that we have been introduced to in leadership, all the varying ways your leadership skills can be measured, *and then* challenge you to think, write, and examine how you are doing. Do you actually know? Are your people happy? What is your retention rate? What is your succession rate, your grievance rate, your production rate? If you want to improve any of these and learn how to really get to *know* the people who work for you, I want to help. You can then work to leverage this information and improve your overall team success.

Just Like the Game of Hockey

Hockey. It's the best analogy I can use to explain this book. So many of us, here in Canada at least, have grown up watching, playing, and coaching the game. Now think back to how players get really good at hockey. First, they probably watch it on TV with a grandparent or parent, then they head out to the local arena or rink to watch siblings and friends play the game on the ice before trying to learn the game themselves. They lace up their first pair of skates (for some of us this is at the age of three or four) and take some skating lessons with a skating coach. Then they suit up with their first equipment: stick, shoulder pads, helmet, shin pads, gloves, and pants. Someone in the change room teaches them how to put each piece on and how to tape up their new stick. Then, onto the ice, they join a team in practice and learn the drills associated with the game. Hours are spent hitting the puck, skating with the puck, passing, and (hopefully) scoring. Coaches are on the ice guiding them as they practice their skills and teaching them how to work with the rest of the team. The coach helps to define each player's role (defence, forward, goalie, centre) and ensures that it suits them. Finally, it's time for their first game. **What happens now is *key*.** Are you anticipating that the coach just says "good luck" and goes home, or should they be sitting on the bench with the team, coaching from the sidelines, giving tips and suggestions as players come off the ice and during intermission? Of course, it would seem ridiculous to just set the players up with a bunch of plays and send them out to play against a team they have never met, in a game that will bring new challenges, new problems to solve and issues they are unfamiliar with. The coach doesn't just assess the game afterward and review hypothetical methods the players could have used to defend the puck or score. No—the coach is there with the team, watching, coaching, encouraging, and providing guidance when players get frustrated and feel ill equipped. So *why* don't we do more of this in leadership? So often it seems leaders are promoted into the role, handed a group of people to "lead and supervise," given a set of expectations and policies, and then wished "good luck." No one is there to coach them. If things go wrong, or you ask for assistance, you are offered a leadership course or a training seminar. It helps, it provides more theoretical insight on what to try and how to do it, but then no one comes on the ice with you after the practice to help assess your efforts. Where are our coaches and consultants? How do we learn to work with our actual team, address the challenges we have with particular players, and figure out how to build trust?

In hockey, good coaches are turned into great coaches by being mentored. In fact, the Canadian Hockey Federation has assessors who sit in the stands, watch the practices and games, watch how the coach interacts with players and how they provide guidance. The assessor then offers the coach real examples and suggestions and works with both players and coaches to improve the team dynamics and win more games. Ken Hitchcock—as mentioned in the Introduction, is a coach known for his success in hockey, coaching other coaches—he emphasizes that "In order to be a really successful coach, you need to build trust in your players. They need to trust you as a coach. You need to build emotional ties with the players. You need to learn to recognize a person's value rather than just their strengths as a player. What do they bring as individuals to the team? Boost hearts and you will boost minds."

Being the Coach I Never Had

This is exactly the role I want to play for you. I want to help you go beyond this book, beyond the courses and the training you have taken. We will discuss leadership strategies and skills you have already developed and learned from so many of the significant leadership books and courses available to you. I am not going to be teaching you how to skate. You already know that. I want to help you expand your knowledge of how to put all the different skills together. Just like in hockey, we need to try some practical drills, on the ice, during the game, in order to get better. We also need to learn *who* your players are. I want to help you improve interactions with your "players." No two teams are the same. Each season, coaches are given a whole new group of people to lead and inspire. You are no different. You change units, departments, personnel, and roles. You may bring with you your skills and experience learned from other years, but you still must learn *who* you are leading. This is not an area that a lot of leadership training has focussed on. I want to give you practical tools and drills you can use.

Think back to my initial example in the introduction about trying to become an effective coach to different people. I had learned lots of "leadership techniques," I excelled at the skills and job I needed to introduce them to, but I had also taken the time to learn *who* they were as trainees. I think this is something we often fail at. We know how to teach people their roles, set expectations, listen with empathy to their concerns, and try to inspire them to "be all they can be," but do we really know *how* to get to know what makes them tick, how they learn, *who* they are, what drives them, what triggers them, and how they address conflict? By teaching you these skills, I will help you to address some of the conflicts and issues that are preventing you from creating and empowering highly functioning teams.

Mini Lessons

The purpose of this book is to share with you the 20 lessons I have learned over the years from people I have been led by, supervised, coached, parented, and worked with. I am not suggesting that I have found all the answers, but my unique experience as a human resources professional, coach, supervisor, mediator, facilitator, and behavioural assessor has enabled me to put a lot of pieces of leadership training and techniques together and answer some of the reason *why* they are not fully working. I intend to be very honest and vulnerable in this book. I will share what I have learned, how I have been judged as a leader, and highlight some of my failures. In doing so, I realize you may not always agree with my interpretation of each situation, the results, or the lessons learned from them. And that's okay. As Brené Brown stated in *Dare to Lead,* "I am taking off my armour. I am going to show you what exists behind the mask. To be willing to rumble with vulnerability, live our values, build trust, and learn to reset, this is part of the rise of daring leader" (75). Together we can re-examine what is working and what isn't.

My Approach

I have approached the writing of this book the same way I would if I were developing a leadership series or two-week training course. I have tried to include a variety of different materials, ways to digest and ponder it, and then various ways to apply it. Just as when you attend a conference or training course, not every method may resonate with you the same way or be presented the way you would have liked to learn it. That's okay. In fact, it is part of the learning we are going to do in this book. Everyone has particular needs and learning styles. For example, when you are in a classroom training session, some participants love the use of videos to bring ideas to life, some love to participate in discussions, while others prefer just to listen and are nauseated by the idea of having to speak up in a group setting. Everyone learns differently. Therefore, I have tried to include many different learning aids in this book that will allow you to digest and process the information the way that you learn. I will also be prompting you to examine how your preferences, assumptions, habits, and traits may impact those around you. Throughout the book, I will encourage you to try different assessment tools, talk out the concepts with friends and colleagues, write out your own definitions for leadership terms, and do some self-reflection. My intent is to have you think about things you already know, introduce new concepts, and rethink ways and reasons you are currently doing things. We will then expand these concepts and apply them to your own leadership role. I will challenge you to think about those around you, the people that work for you, in a new way.

For example:

- Do you know how each of them prefers to learn?
- Do you expect that all of your teammates will want to participate in meetings the same way?
- Are you asking them to perform in their preferred work style or yours?
- How is this impacting your discussions and the generation of new ideas?

Coaching from the Bleachers

This book will encourage you to look at many aspects of your own leadership, your behaviours, and the subsequent impact on others. It will also give you new strategies and tools to incorporate so that you can measure and assess not only how you are doing, but what to do if things go astray. However, as a human resources professional and trained mediator, I also recognize the need to sometimes have someone else step in to help you guide the relationships—allowing you to get back on track, improve communication, and develop new ideas and strategies. Therefore, as the book progresses, I will also explore the role and advantage of using an organizational mediator, coach, and consultant as part of your leadership strategy. Too often we take the training, read the book, and that's it. Back to work we go, and it seems very little changes. Leadership, self-awareness, building relationships, holding people accountable for behaviours, responding to workplace conflict, and trying to develop employees is hard work. Sometimes you need to have the ability to call someone up, ask for objective advice, get some one-on-one coaching, bring in someone to help mediate the issues, and offer your team specific training to address their needs.

Getting to the Root of the Issues

My goal is to help you understand the *why* that exists at the root of most issues. I want to help set you up for success and then help coach you along the journey to get there. I will introduce tools you can use, ways that you can utilize this book and implement action plans. You can use my assessment tools to learn more about yourself and those you lead. You can learn from my mistakes and institute your own new practices. In doing so, you will build your own leadership skills in a practical and specific way. You will learn how to address issues by getting to the root of what is causing them.

At the end of the book, I will also speak to how I have developed ways to take the learning beyond the book, helping organizations and leaders deal with "real life issues," and further all our learning. When tough situations arise, you can use the tools from the book, and even reach out to me to discuss them "mid-game." I have created a business entitled Inspiring Organizational Growth to enable me to design ways to support leaders and their teams during their growth process. In some scenarios we may need to just chat it out, or I can even meet with you and your team, learn about everyone's skills and behaviours, and then observe the team at "play." I will watch the game from the "stands," make notes on which players are dominating the "puck" or issue, which ones are holding back, and who may need to develop further skills in certain areas. I can help to design a training program for the whole team, or just particular "players." If you have a couple of players that seem to have conflicting personalities or opinions on how the game should be played, we can deal with that. We can also address the "gossiping and backstabbing" that may be occurring in the change room and off the ice that is impacting how well your team gels and plays on the ice. We can learn together as leaders and improve your leadership, your team, and help reach your "goals." Together we can build needed trust and inspire needed conversations. In no time, you and your team will be scoring goals and winning championships!

Ready to start approaching leadership the same way we would any other skill set? Then please join me in learning more about yourself and those you lead.

LESSON 2

We Are Missing the Key Link
Not Another #$!% Leadership Course

An email pops up on your work computer screen. *Senior management is inviting you to register for the upcoming leadership training seminar—a three-day training course on how to become a more effective leader in the organization.*

Your immediate reaction is (let's be honest ...):

a. Oh yeah! I have been waiting for a course like this!
b. Are you #$!% kidding me? Why don't they take their own course and learn how to lead?
c. I don't have time for this *#!&. Just another flavour of the month. We never use any of it.
d. Hmm. Wonder if they will teach us anything new? Leadership is hard work, and all the theories don't seem to pan out when I try them with real employees.

To be honest, I have had all four of these reactions. Back in the early-mid 2000s, I was excited to take any and every course offered. I read all the leadership books I could get my hands on. I even became the facilitator who *sent* you those emails and ran the leadership and supervisory training courses. I was excited about organizational change management, learning all the leadership styles, conflict resolution styles, leadership strategies, and more. I had all my books highlighted and tabbed for quick reference, and I loved mentoring new leaders, coaches, trainers, and supervisors on how they could effectively build and develop others. The concepts of leadership training are good and well researched. Lean methodology found in *The Toyota Way to Lean Leadership* by Jeffrey K. Liker emphasized what I was striving for:

> The Toyota View is that every organization must identify and solve its own challenges based on the variables of its process, place, people, and any other unique factors. The role of the leader in this context is to be open to the kind of self development needed to cultivate her own leadership skills, develop subordinates so that they can grow and improve, and remove obstacles and set challenges and goals so that teams at all levels of the organization can contribute to Toyota's continuous improvement and attainment of its long term goals. (Liker 16)

Then I hit a time in my career when doubt started to creep in. Why did it seem that over and over leaders seem to be frustrated by the same things? When I met with other leaders, they all spoke of how their organizations presented new processes, a new theme, each time they got a new executive leader. Everyone seemed to send the junior leaders on the course, but often the boss was too busy to attend, or said they *had already met with the presenter and understood the material. Why* after taking the training, and having the inevitable follow up strategic meetings on how the group planned to move the organization forward and implement these new strategies and ideas, did it seem like absolutely nothing really changed? People complained that their leaders often seem to lead the same way they always had; no one was listening to new ideas or considering other people's priorities or input, and morale was down. The more I continued to facilitate and discuss these ideas with other professionals, I found I could no longer ignore participants' frustrations and contempt for the new training. *Why are we learning this?* they would ask. *How are we going to use this?* I felt frustrated too. I had read so many books by brilliant authors and business leaders. I had listened to their podcasts and TED Talks. I knew that what they were teaching was valuable and played key roles in leaders learning more about their own leadership style, their strengths, their default behaviours. Self-improvement, vulnerability, curiosity, and the willingness to expand and change are vital in leadership. These are all vital components to effective leadership. **So why was it so hard to implement those things in real life, with real employees, in real organizations?** Why do leaders often feel like they are running backwards on a treadmill, not able to keep up with growing demands, low morale, low retention, conflicts with employees, and growing frustrations? What were we missing? What was I *not* teaching people? What was the missing link to effective leadership?

Market Research

As a leader, coach, and supervisor of more than 25 years, I started to do my own external market research. I wanted to better understand what employees, from an assortment of occupations (mining, teaching, nursing, human resources, government, etc) , were looking for in an effective leaderand how we as leaders could meet these needs. I had met many organizations filled with wonderful employees, leaders, coaches, and trainers. I had seen many great examples of effective leadership. I knew it existed. As a human resources professional, I had also met with other organizations who seemed to have examples of both effective and ineffective leadership. I knew that it wasn't enough to just send people on more training to develop the needed skills, or discipline people for not getting along, or let disgruntled employees simply leave the organization and find another job, or worse yet, having mismanaged people stay with the organization and poison the culture. We all love our organizations too much to let this continue to happen. So what are we all missing? How can we effectively improve things?

To try and gain further perspective on this, I conducted a survey to learn more about the current experience people are having in their workforces. I asked participants, who ranged from students in their first job to professionals in many different work fields, to answer a series of questions on *what makes an effective leader?* The responses I got were riveting and have contributed to the development of this book.

Here are the first three questions and their corresponding responses. As you read the questions, think also about how you would answer them.

1. Do you enjoy working for/with your current supervisor or coach?

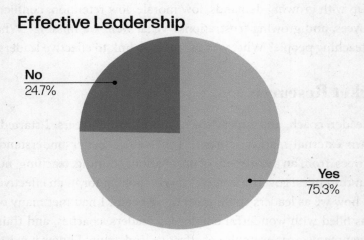

2. What qualities do you *most* admire in an effective supervisor/coach?

- Compassion, respect, integrity, knowledge, empathy, trust, authenticity, humility
- Effective communication skills, effective listener
- Transparent, understanding, fair, flexible, supportive, approachable
- Able to make a decision, open to hearing others' opinions
- Respect for their subordinates, willingness to elevate their employees
- Empowering, calm, determined, wise, patient
- Willing to push you, prepare you for the worst so you are more than ready for the best
- Leads by example
- Willing to have difficult honest conversations

- Sense of humour and willingness to be human

3. What qualities do you *least* admire in a supervisor/coach?

- Ego, saying one thing and doing another
- Dismissiveness, micromanagement, intolerance, lack of support
- Arrogance, poor communication, lack of vision, inability to change
- Impatient, controlling, shaming, belittling
- Rigid thinking, dishonesty, coercive, non-transparent, hypocritical
- Stepping on others to get ahead
- Favouritism, nepotism, or discrimination
- Doesn't stand behind their employees
- Unavailable, hard to reach—doesn't return phone calls or emails
- Talking as opposed to listening, doesn't listen before getting angry
- Lacking in trust, not a team player
- Lack of empathy
- Disorganized, lacking in their own confidence
- Underestimates employees and their abilities
- Takes all the credit, doesn't empower others

These first three responses demonstrate the need for organizations to offer leaders enhanced self-awareness training, communication skills, and inclusion training. But they also illustrate that it isn't enough to just tell them to read a book or sit through a three-day seminar on "being an effective leader." We need to determine how to enable them to transfer this knowledge into action.

Recognizing Your Own Behavioural Traits

We all know that leaders must be willing to recognize their own strengths, identify their weaknesses, admit to their "go to behaviours," and be willing to challenge themselves to examine how they impact others. However, as leaders, do we really do it?

The survey asked respondents:

Is your supervisor/coach open to suggestions/feedback offered to improve their leadership style?

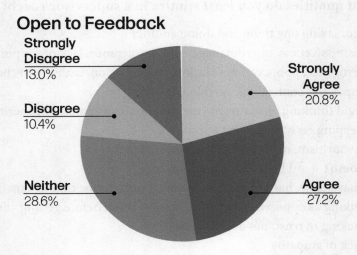

Open to Feedback

Strongly Disagree 13.0%

Strongly Agree 20.8%

Disagree 10.4%

Neither 28.6%

Agree 27.2%

Responses:

AGREE/STRONGLY AGREE

- Good leaders see self-improvement as a sign of good leadership
- Good leaders are able to give and take criticisms and suggestions
- Good leaders ask for feedback
- Good leaders openly acknowledge if they don't know something and show appreciation for learning

DISAGREE/UNKNOWN

- There is no room for feedback or discussion from staff regarding concerning management
- Ageism: leaders are young and arrogant and don't appreciate hearing the opinions from older/wiser people
- More of a dictatorship—"do as I say"—and suggestions are unwanted
- Decisions are final and cannot be questioned
- I have never tried
- Some leaders are open to feedback and others definitely are *not*

- Not my place to tell a supervisor how to do their job; stay silent
- Suggestions viewed as threats
- Help offered to the organization is turned down

These responses will challenge you to really think about how you have tackled your own growth and whether your team feels safe enough to tell you their thoughts.

I have a series of other survey responses that are highlighted in upcoming lessons on conflict, teamwork, performance ratings, retention, and trust building. The responses to each of these questions give us insight into areas that are examined in this book. They reveal elements of how employees feel, why they share, and why they don't. Read the comments carefully. Some are very hard to hear as leaders, but they offer important lessons.

Why Issues Arise

I have always loved learning more about behavioural science and the study of human interactions. My undergrad in psychology and law was both intriguing and challenging. It started me on a path of discovery into what causes conflict, how people associate behaviours with their own values and beliefs, and how people's identity and history contribute to who they are. To learn more, I also took a long and intensive series of mediation courses to become a mediator. I saw it as another potential tool or skill I could use in learning to help answer some of these questions. It helped me better understand why issues arise between people and what needs to happen to resolve those same issues. It also enabled me to have some fairly significant *Ah-ha!* moments. All of the sudden, training and concepts I had learned earlier on—behaviour, needs, interests, styles, and skills—started to move together like puzzle pieces. I re-evaluated training courses I had run, issues I had dealt with, employees I seemed unable to help, and I realized key things I had missed. I suddenly realized that to really learn how to lead, and engage the learning we already have, we as leaders needed to develop ways to transfer what we had learned to the *real people* we were leading. We need to learn how to figure out *who* they are. I have created this book to enable you, as leaders, to do just that.

Getting Started

The premise of this book is to engage the effective leader that you are, and help you understand that all your skills, training, and effort are valuable. The piece many of us have missed, however, is this: **Do you know *who* you are leading and how this can help you in effectively inspiring them?** If you don't know *who* they are, then trying to introduce new processes won't work. You need to understand how they may react, why, and how to build trust. It's not an easy or quick fix solution, but with effort it can have amazing results. After all, 100% of the respondents in my survey indicated that *how you lead will impact the success or failure of your team.*

Being an Effective Leader

If we go back to the hockey analogy, a really good coach has taken the time to get to know their players and what makes them tick. They know which players function best under pressure and use them on the power plays. They also know when to pull them off the ice, recognizing they are triggered, and help to prevent them from getting a retaliatory penalty because they are frustrated with the other team. An effective coach is there after the game to provide a recap, encourage discussion, and help the players work through their frustrations with each other and the other team. The better they know their team, the better the team works.

Being an effective coach doesn't, however, mean you are there to give them all the answers or provide all the solutions. Instead, you are there to mediate, facilitate, and empower them to communicate with you and one another so they can work together and find their own solutions. If you are trying to help them with their own professional development, train them in new skills, guide their career path, or have them work more effectively with others, then you have to get to know them—really know them—first. Build trust, admit to your own mistakes, recognize your own tendencies and behaviours, and ask for help when needed. Leadership is a lifelong journey, but well worth the ride.

LESSON 3

See Yourself Clearly

Who Are You?

To understand the value of really getting to know the people we lead, we need to first understand ourselves. This is not an easy task and, in fact, amounts to a lifelong journey. It is also not one you can do on your own. In order to truly assess *who* you are, you will need to become vulnerable and willing to share your findings and insight with others whom you trust. People who have worked with you and for you. But first, let's work on learning more about you.

Many of you will have already done some work on learning *who you are* during your previous leadership training sessions. You may have done a DISC profile assessment, a Myers-Briggs Type Indicator, a CliftonStrengths assessment, a quiz on your conflict styles, your learning styles, your behavioural traits, your triggers, and more. I want you to find those assessments and re-read what they say. All that content and information is vital to developing a better understanding of how you interact with others. If you don't have these results or can't remember which one of your many leadership courses and binders they might be in, that's okay too. We are going to work through many of the concepts right here in this book. I will reintroduce you to ones you may have seen and encourage you to try new ones. One such assessment is called the Predictive Index Behavioural Assessment. It will provide you with a deeper understanding of not only who you are, but who you may prefer to work with, and who you may find more challenging to work with and lead.

Behaviours and Drives

I first took the training to become a Predictive Index Behavioural Practitioner in 2019. I was ready for a change. I needed to add a new element to my personal growth and wanted to learn more about how we could attract, train, mentor, and retain effective employees. As a human resources professional, I knew that employees are the heartbeat of the organization. I wanted employees to feel valued, ensure their interests were being heard and met, and increase the chance they would stay with their organization. So I needed to find a way to learn more about them and then share this information with their coach, trainer, colleagues, and supervisor so that we could develop plans on how to work more effectively together.

Are you already cringing? Are you about to put the book down and say, *just another flavour of the month, another assessment, another tool*? Wondering why you should believe or even learn any of this? You wouldn't be the first to have this reaction when hearing about Predictive Indexing (PI). I have had lots of eye rolls and disinterested stares when I talk excitedly about PIs. I get it. I am not trying to sell you on a new concept. I promise! I just want to illustrate how I have utilized this tool to learn information that made my job as a leader much easier. As you read through this next portion, you may also determine ways you can better utilize your own existing assessment tools. Used effectively they can provide needed insight into how and *why* things are happening. Finally, you might be able to answer some of those questions that keep you up at night.

- *Why* did Jillian get so angry in that meeting today?
- *Why* won't Bill engage with his coworkers?
- *Why* can't Myriam just follow my directions and complete her reports the way I need them done?
- *Why* can't we seem to hire the right person for that position?

Using a Predictive Analysis Tool

In his book *Predicting Success,* David Lahey explains how the PI assessment tool can be used by leaders to effectively engage, assess, and communicate with those they are leading. Developed in the 1950s, the tool has been validated and utilized to assess millions of users. It can help organizations with a variety of management strategies, including employee selection, onboarding, employee engagement, leadership development, team building, enhancing organizational culture, and resolving conflict.

The assessment presents participants with an analytical report of their behaviour: how they behave, what drives them, and how others expect them to behave. The variance between the two domains of what drives a person and how they think people expect them to behave provides helpful insight into daily workplace interactions. Think about instances at work when you may feel pressured to "be someone you are not." Assessments can help people better understand why they are struggling with certain tasks or strongly dislike interacting with certain people. The reports can help illustrate how similar and, at times, dissimilar people can be. Using this information helps leaders understand why conflicts arise, why there can be differences in expectations, learning strategies, and job fit amongst a set of employees.

The Behavioural Assessment Report

Similar to other assessment tools, the PI generates a Behavioural Assessment Report that includes three graphs. The Self graph describes default behaviour and need preferences. This graph is your base line. Left to your own devices, your own preferences, this is how you would show up in the world and how you would interact with others. It is also how you will tend to behave when you are under stress and/or feeling uncomfortable. You will always go back to your default behaviour. Think about it, if you are put in an uncomfortable situation, given a new work assignment, assigned to work with a new group of people that you don't know very well, how will you behave?

The second graph is your Self-Concept graph. This is the one that best depicts how you think others want you to behave in that new setting. Are you perceiving the need to be quiet, sit and listen, and not ask any questions? Or do you think they want you to be interactive and socializing with everyone? Do you have a preference? This is the graph that best describes how you are trying to "push" yourself to behave and meet the expectations of others—but how long can you last before you return to your default behaviours?

That is what graph three, the Synthesis, best describes. It shows how far you will predictively be able to stretch yourself, abandon your own comfort zone, and strive to meet the needs of others. Some areas are easier to stretch than others. We may be able to force ourselves to politely participate in that social interaction for an hour before we are bored of it and want to go back and sit at our desk. Other areas, however, are even harder to expand. Things like how much interest you have in listening to someone's detailed explanation of their camping adventures or their play by play on steps they took in purchasing a new car. Some people are just naturally more prone to providing and needing details, while others just want the Coles Notes version of the events. In a work environment, this may translate to just how much detail you need from your employees. How much do you want them to tell you? How do you want them to present the information to you?

The Behavioural Report can provide a lot of insight into why you find it easier to work with certain people more than others. Why you enjoy certain tasks more than other duties? The more you can learn about yourself, the more you will be able to, in a very practical sense, discover what you need to be aware of and how you may be impacting others in your efforts to lead them.

Taking the Assessment

The PI assessment itself is very easy to complete. It typically takes less than 10 minutes. If you are curious, you can go to my website to find a link: www.inspiringorganizationalgrowth.ca. You may be intrigued on how well it describes you. I have sat with many people who, after doing their assessment, are a little surprised by the accuracy of the results.

I have used these reports to generate some great new discussions among leaders and their coworkers. Often the first insight people have is not work related, but instead relates more to their personal and family life. Suddenly, they can understand why they and their life partner approach the planning of a trip or the renovating of their house *very* differently! The beauty of the assessment is that it also emphasizes that neither person is wrong. One personality construct is not superior to or better than another. We are just different and unique in our construct.

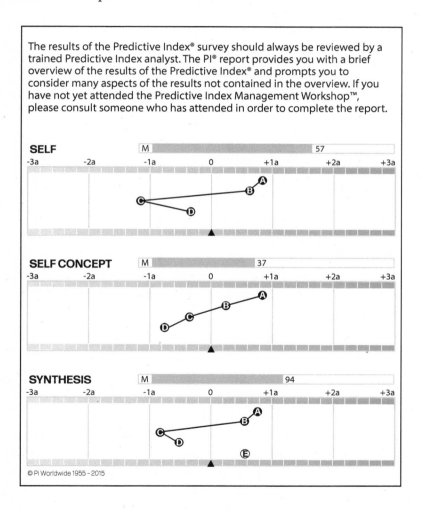

Example of a Behavioural Report

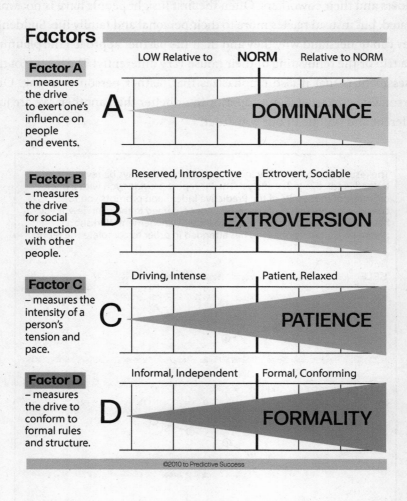

Factors

Factor A
– measures the drive to exert one's influence on people and events.

A — LOW Relative to | NORM | Relative to NORM — **DOMINANCE**

Factor B
– measures the drive for social interaction with other people.

B — Reserved, Introspective | Extrovert, Sociable — **EXTROVERSION**

Factor C
– measures the intensity of a person's tension and pace.

C — Driving, Intense | Patient, Relaxed — **PATIENCE**

Factor D
– measures the drive to conform to formal rules and structure.

D — Informal, Independent | Formal, Conforming — **FORMALITY**

©2010 to Predictive Success

Explaining Your Results

As you can see, each of the graphs—Self, Self-Concept, and Synthesis—also have letters assigned to their graph points. My preference is to use the letters (A, B, C, D) for now, and not their descriptive title of A=Dominance, B=Extroversion, C=Patience, and D=Formality. I have learned over the years as a facilitator that language and the words we use can really trigger people. The same can potentially occur when you look at the words Dominance, Extroversion, Patience, and Formality and start to add meaning to them. Therefore, I would ask that you approach them with an open mind. If you are not loving the idea of finding out how "dominant" you like to be, or if you are not comfortable with the term "patience," then just refer to these qualities by their letters. *Where is my A, where is my C in comparison to other people around me?*

For the sake of clarity, I have provided you with a brief description of what each driving factor refers to:

A—Dominance: This measures how much you want to have influence over others in making decisions. Are you comfortable taking the lead and making decisions on your own? The further your Dominance (A) moves in the left of the scale indicates the less you want to make decisions on your own and would prefer to collaborate with others or be led by others. The further right your A moves on the scale, the more comfortable you are in taking command and making decisions.

The same is true for the other three drives.

B—Extroversion: This measures how much of a need you have to socially interact with others. The further to the left your results are, the more you enjoy and need to have time on your own for introspection. The further to the right your B glides on the scale, the more you enjoy and need to socialize with other people to feel fulfilled.

C—Patience: This measures how much you enjoy and need a change in pace and predictability. If your Patience (C) is far to the left, you really need to have change, to be driven to try new challenges, and become bored and uninterested if things remain predictable and stagnant. On the other hand, if your C is far to the right of the scale, you enjoy having steadfast work, predictable assignments, and routine.

D—Formality: This measures the drive you have for formality, rules, and structure. The further your Formality (D) moves to the left, the more you enjoy the ability to be autonomous, to take charge of your own work, and to find flexibility in how you conduct yourself. If your D is further to the right, you really enjoy structure, policies, rules, and find it hard to operate in ambiguous situations.

As I am sure you can imagine, there are many versions and variances to how the results will play out for different participants. Therefore, Predictive Index has also broken similar profiles down into *seventeen different personality profiles* that further help people acknowledge and take pride in how they approach the world, tasks, relationships, and interactions with others. It will also help you to understand which profiles you are most similar to, and which ones will provide potential challenges to you due to the fact that they approach their work and their world very differently than you do.[2] For me, one of the key takeaways from the personality profile is its ability to highlight your strengths and cautionary behaviours. The assessment is not saying you have *strengths* and *weaknesses*, but it does highlight how some of your strengths may cause issues or moments of concern for people whose strengths are different than your own. This is a very important concept that I will explore much deeper as we proceed in the book. I have personally witnessed how people learning this information about themselves are then able to do a lot of self-reflection into why certain interactions in their past may have occurred the way they did.

Sharing My Profile

Before I ask anyone to be vulnerable and discuss their results with me, I always share with them a little bit about me and who I am. I find as a facilitator and leader that if I can show people that I am willing to be vulnerable, then it helps to build trust and expand just how willing they may open up to me.

So here we go …

I am a **Maverick**, which clearly explains why I was so excited to finally write this book, expand on who we are as leaders, and how we can assist others in developing their own skill sets.

---

2   You will find your Profile Description at the top right of your Behavioural Report. I have included a brief description of each on my website www.inspiringorganizationalgrowth.ca.

Someone with a **Maverick** personality profile is characterized as innovative, goal oriented, visionary, and flexible. Graphically I look like this:

As you can see, my A is to the far right of the graph, meaning I am comfortable taking risks and making decisions.

My B is also on the right side of the graph, meaning I enjoy socializing and interacting with others. As a learner I would be defined as "interpersonal."

My C, however, is to the left of the graph. That means I enjoy having flexibility and changing priorities.

My D is also to the far left of the graph, illustrating that I am not highly motivated by structure and rules. I want to challenge the status quo and ask "Why do we do it this way? Can we do better?"

Mavericks are visionaries who want to achieve what's never been achieved before. They are not fans of the status quo. They want to shake things up. They tend to be innovative, influential, daring, and direct with a tolerance for taking risks. They are natural leaders. They can be task oriented and persistent. They thrive when given a goal and the freedom to determine how to achieve that goal.

Natural Strengths:

- Innovative
- Goal oriented
- Visionary
- Flexible

Common Drivers:

- Opportunities to influence
- Freedom from rules and controls
- Variety
- Competition

Cautionary Behaviours (things I struggle with):

- I am not a fan of technical work
- I have a limited attention for detail
- I will delegate work and have loose follow up
- I may appear as tough-minded

So what do you think? I know, some of you are already cringing. I would *not* be your ideal choice for a teammate or employee. If some of my fellow colleagues and supervisors are reading this book, they are likely nodding their heads in agreement.

Now Think about the *Why*

1. Are you detail oriented? Would my lack of need for detail and follow through stress you out.?
2. Do you have a direct leadership style? Does my need to ask "why?" rather than just say "yes, I will do that" seem annoying?
3. Are you more reserved/introverted than I am? Does the idea of collaborating in meetings or being asked your opinion in a public setting makes you nauseous and want to avoid me?
4. Are you more steadfast than I am? Does my lack of need for process and routine causes you to feel stressed and anxious?

What if You Were My Supervisor?

1. If you had this information about me beforehand, would you pick me for your team?
2. Would your team/unit get along with me, or would there be friction? Why or why not?
3. Would having this information about my needs, behaviours, and traits help you to guide me, supervise me, and lead me? Why or why not?
4. Would my lack of detail in reports and failure to edit my work lead you to believe I am lazy, disorganized, and/or lacking in skill?
5. Have you had previous experiences trying to lead a **Maverick**? Did you enjoy it?

Learning to Challenge Our Assumptions and Comfort Level

These are all the types of questions we are going to explore in the next few lessons. There is a lot to unpack about ourselves, our previous leadership training, who we like and dislike to work with, and how using this information can help us find the missing links we are looking for. Whether it is trying to lead your own unit more effectively, trying to attract and retain more employees, diversify your workforce, or deal with the ongoing issues of low morale and grievances, this book is designed to enlighten and potentially help you find some of the answers you are looking for.

In his book *Failing Forward,* John C. Maxwell teaches the reader how to turn mistakes into stepping stones. I have read this book several times during my leadership journey. He lovingly illustrates that in order to move forward, we must follow this process:

1. See yourself clearly
2. Admit your flaws honestly
3. Discover your strengths joyfully
4. Build on your strengths passionately (93)

In order to do this, let's start with your own personality profile. Read your Behavioural Report.[3]

- What are your strengths?
- What are the associated challenges for others when presented with those strengths?
- What are your cautionary behaviours?
- How do you best interact with others?
- What might this mean about your preferred leadership style?

We will be referring to how you operate, your self concept, and your default self behaviours and traits throughout the book. You are welcome to pull this information from a PI report or other assessments you have already completed. The purpose is to examine who you are, how you lead, how you can impact trust, inspire teams, and effect organizational success.

---

3   If you have not already done so, I encourage you to take some time and try it by going to the link found on my website www. inspiringorganizationalgrowth.ca. Learn more about yourself, your needs, and your behaviours.

LESSON 4

Diving Deep into Your Preferred Leadership Style

Turning Mistakes into Victories

How do you define effective leadership? What does that term mean to you when it comes to behaviours, ethics, processes, and styles?

If you are like me, you will have read and listened to dozens of books and podcasts on this very topic. In fact, if you look, there have been millions of books, courses, and podcasts written and developed to address leadership. The podcast *Read to Lead* by Jeff Brown is a fantastic resource you can use to learn more about new and upcoming books on leadership and leadership concepts. Each book, although focused on similar nonfiction subject matter, allows the reader/listener to learn and challenge themselves on new concepts or re-examine old ones. Leadership is evolving. You would think that concepts of the past would fade away and be replaced by new, more progressive ones in which leaders truly wanted to empower their employees to be themselves and prosper. So *why* do so many leaders seem to fall back into the same old adages of command and control, direct leadership, and authoritarian leadership based on "do as I say"? I would suggest it is because they don't yet have the tools to offset the reaction or behaviour.

You have just finished studying the science behind behavioural index-ing. We have learned that people have their own set of strengths and cautionary behaviours. Leaders are not different. However, armed with this information, leaders can learn how to incorporate new methodologies, tools, and strategies to offset their need to revert to their cautionary behaviours. For example, if a leader knows they are likely to default to a command-and-control style when faced with situations that are lacking in detail or structure, what could they do to proactively prevent this type of situation from occurring? Additionally, when a situation does occur, how can they better explain their needs to others before they react? These are the types of questions we will explore.

What Is Effective Leadership?

First, we need to determine what is effective leadership. If any of you have had to take a fundamentals of leadership course, or written a management exam, you will know that there is always a section on leadership theories and styles. I will be honest. Not being a verbal learner, or one who can simply read and digest the information without putting it into a practical context or discussion, I often floundered trying to contextually apply the concepts on my own. I would have to try to label them in the book I was reading, write down examples from my life experience, connecting different leaders to different styles. *Note to self: Don't leave your labelled book out for anyone to find!* I used to display many of my books on a table at the back of my classroom for participants to refer to on break. I remember the terrifying day someone picked up one of those books and I suddenly remembered that their name was associated with one of the coloured tabs I had added to the book! Needless to say, all tabs were removed after that!

Over the years, I have realized that each time I go back, re-read one of my books, or teach another course, I am able to learn more, apply new examples, and relate to the concepts on a deeper level. Why? Because leadership is a journey. The book *Becoming a Resonant Leader* by Anne McKee, Richard Boyatzis, and Frances Johnston is a great example of one such book. This is a book on transformational leadership that challenges you to "wrestle with profound aspects of yourself as a person and as a leader so that you can become more resonant, develop your emotional intelligence, renew your relationships, and sustain your effectiveness" (1–2). It goes on to say that a resonant leader is attuned to themselves and the needs, desires, and dreams of the people they lead.

As we move on, we are going to be examining the type of leader you want to emulate and *why*. What is important to you? How do you want to appear to those you lead? Are there areas you want to change or improve, or are you satisfied with how you relate to others?

Perhaps your motivation to grow and change will be a financial one. Statistics show us that people leave leaders, not organizations. In fact, 64% of my survey respondents have left organizations due to their supervisors, and 10% are currently considering it. The cost of attracting, retaining, and developing new employees impacts production, morale, and the bottom line. These are statistics we can't afford to ignore.

Have You Ever Left an Organization Because of Supervision?

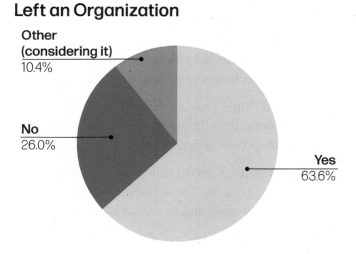

Left an Organization

Other (considering it) 10.4%

No 26.0%

Yes 63.6%

Definitions and Styles

There are *many* different leadership styles to consider; however, I have designed an exercise that will have you explore six styles and think about how they relate to you and others around you. As you read each one, you may start to think of other layers and concepts that also come into play. How self-aware is someone of their own leadership style? Do some leadership styles require more emotional intelligence and self-awareness than others? Do some require the leader to be less self-absorbed and more altruistic than others? Do some leaders seem to move fluidly between styles, while others are more stringent and comfortable with only one or two? Why?

Autocratic Leadership—Through this command-and-control type of leadership, leaders tend to make decisions without requiring or asking for the input of others.

Authoritative Leadership—While similar to autocratic, these leaders take the time to explain their ideas with great confidence. They set goals and objectives for others to follow, explaining all processes, and overseeing the steps it will take to get there.

Democratic Leadership—These leaders enjoy engaging their followers. They share information that will impact work responsibilities and ask for input or opinions before choosing a course of action.

Laissez-Faire Leadership—This leadership style involves very little oversight. These leaders allow their people to make their own decisions and take charge of their own assignments.

Pacemaking Leadership—A leadership style very effective in getting things done and driving results, These leaders set the bar high, are very driven, set timelines and deadlines to ensure work is completed.

Servant Leadership—Servant leaders aim to develop leadership qualities in others. They promote innovation, empower others, and have a stewardship philosophy. They are committed to the growth and success of others. (Martinuzzi, 2021)

Let's start by doing a short exercise to identify some of your own preferences when it comes to leadership. *Remember, these answers are for your eyes only, so you may want to write them on a separate piece of paper and not directly in the book![4]*

Using the table below, start to think about leaders that have had an impact, good or bad, on your life. They could have been coaches, parents, colleagues, supervisors, teachers, mentors, or friends. They may have impressed you, either positively or negatively, with the way they conducted themselves in a certain situation or had an overall lasting impression on you. Challenge yourself to think about *why* they had that impact. What was it they did or said that allows you now to label their leadership style? You may decide to list more than one style for the same leader. Think about the situation. Did one style work more effectively than another?

The interesting part of this exercise is that it starts to help unpack not only what we each admire in a leader, but it also reveals that each of us may need different things from the same leader. For example, think of someone that has coached you in the past. Now look at the leadership styles. Although several readers may have had the same coach, they may have wanted different things from that person. Some will therefore list the person as an effective leader/coach, while others will consider them ineffective.

---

4   You can print or download all of the tables and exercises found in this book from my website: www.inspiringorganizationalgrowth.ca.

Leaders in Your Life and How They Lead:

Name	Style and Situation	Effective or Ineffective	Why?
Example: Jim Doe	*Authoritative— meeting on Monday*	*Ineffective*	*I didn't get to ask any questions, so I don't understand why we are moving in this direction*

The beauty of doing an exercise like this is that it often creates more questions than answers. It is designed to start you on a deeper dive into your own leadership styles, preferences, behaviours, and defaults. Our PI assessment from Lesson 3 enlightens us to the fact that no matter how hard we try, under stress we tend to revert to default behaviours unless we are able to take the time to recognize them and purposefully alter our behaviour choices. This concept of adaptation and growth is also the premise of the concept of emotional intelligence that Daniel Goldman introduced to many of us in his 1995 book *Emotional Intelligence*. In order to grow and build your strengths, you need to apply self-awareness, self-discipline, and empathy to how you interact with the world.

Now look at the names of the leaders you have chosen to highlight in your table. What if you then also rated their willingness to grow from experiences? Before answering that question, you need to take care when you do this part of the exercise. My human resources training has shown me the cautionary risks and biases that come with asking people to do ratings. You need to ensure that you are rating the person in a totality of experiences and not just the most recent, the best, the worst, or in comparison to others.

Rater Bias

To reduce rater bias, leaders must be cognizant of the risks that occur, often at a conscious or unconscious level. These may include:

1. **Recency Bias:** The rating of someone's overall performance based solely on a recent event or interaction (Last week they did great.) (Yesterday they were late!)

2. **Halo Bias:** The rating of someone's overall performance based solely on one positive event or interaction (They did a great job on that one project.)

3. **Horn Bias:** The rating of someone's overall performance based solely on one negative event or interaction (They did so poorly on that one assignment.)

4. **Similarity or Affinity Bias:** The rating of someone's overall performance is biased or impacted by the rater's similarity to them (We went to the same school, have the same background, worked in the same unit.)

5. **Contrast/Comparison Bias:** The rating of someone's overall performance in contrast /comparison to another person (This employee is more effective at A than B is; therefore, they should get a higher rating.)

6. **Leniency Bias:** The rating of someone's overall performance is better than it should be based on their performance indicators (I like them. They are a nice person; I didn't want to cause waves or upset them, so I rated them higher than I should have.)

Taking all these potential rating biases into consideration, look over the names of the leaders you have selected. In general, based on several examples and insights you have on them:

1. Do you think they have a willingness to grow and change?
2. Does their willingness to grow matter to you? Why or why not?

Who Do You Want to Emulate?

Now for the difficult part of this exercise. We have spent time thinking about those around us, what we like and don't like, what we treasure about their leadership styles and hope to emulate, and things we hope to avoid. Now it is time to rate ourselves. Using the same type of table, take some time to write down examples of your own leadership. The more specific you can be in the situations—what was happening at the time for you emotionally, situationally, and *who* it was you were leading—will enable the learning to be that much more effective. Again, don't fall victim to the rating bias. Try not only to think of examples from last week, or your best examples, your worst examples, ones from only an isolated environment (work or home). The more expansive you can be in your examples, people, and situations, the more you will get from the   exercise.

Person Involved	Situation	My Leadership Style	Effective/ Ineffective

Just as we stated in the coaching example, different people may have different takes on the same situation. Look at the names of the people you have listed. What do you think they would say if you asked them to fill in this table for the same situation? Would they label it as the same leadership style? Was it effective or ineffective for them and why? Do you know? If you did, would it help you grow?

Expanding Your Leadership Style

For me, this is the most exciting part of the leadership journey, and the one most of us have skipped. We have taken the leadership courses, learned about the different styles, reflected on whose leadership we want to emulate, and even critiqued our own leadership successes and failures, but we haven't asked those around us to do the same.

- *Why* do you think this is true?
- How many of us are willing to be vulnerable and show courage to ask these tough questions?
- What could we learn if we did?

Brené Brown, in her book *Dare to Lead,* calls it the willingness to rumble. She defines a *rumble* as "a discussion, conversation or meeting defined by a commitment to lean into vulnerability, to stay curious and generous, to stick with the messy middle of problem identification and solving, to take a break and circle back when necessary, to be fearless in owning our parts, and demonstrate our willingness to remove our armour and be vulnerable" (10).

Think back to the hockey analogy from Lesson 1. A great coach is willing to sit with their team in the locker room and talk out what worked and what didn't. For this discussion to be effective and meaningful, everyone has to be vulnerable and curious about how they could have played differently, impacted the plays differently, or led differently. It's not enough to just talk about hypothetical plays: "In the second period, we should have gotten on the puck sooner; we should have guarded against that defensive play they used three times to get the puck out of their end." You need to name players who were on the ice at the time, who should have been on the play, whether the coach made a poor line change or failed to explain a play properly. That's the only way you are going to improve the next time you face the same team. So why don't we do this more often in our work settings? How often do you sit down and *rumble* with your team?

Locker Room Debriefs

If you were the hockey coach, how would you want your "locker room debrief" to go? How would you want it to sound? What would you want to say? What impact would you want to have? Look at your first list of leaders and what you admired/didn't admire about them. If you had been able to sit down and debrief with them, and been able to share your insight and thoughts about how they *led* the interaction, what would you have said? Did you enjoy their approach, or are there things you wish they had done differently? *Why?*

Now take your second list. As we move through this book, I am going to challenge you to debrief with one of the people on that list. As we move into the next few lessons, you will realize there are a few more things you need to learn before you can risk asking someone to be that vulnerable with you. Much of the trust you will need will have to be developed long before the *rumble* can take place and be effective. But for now, just keep this concept of a rumble in mind. Who would you like to talk to? What would you like to learn? What would you like to share?

PART 2

—

WHO ARE YOU LEADING?

LESSON 5

Judging Others =
Missed Opportunities

The Risk of Mislabelling

*T*he *End of Average* by Todd Rose challenges us to think about who
we are hiring and what expectations we hold for them. Do we have
expectations of who our employees need to be? Do we want them to fit
within specific parameters we have designed when it comes to their performance, how they conduct themselves, how they fit into our teams and
our organization? This is a concept we will explore throughout this book
in different ways. We will look at the biases we may hold when it comes
to how someone should perform. What labels do we use to describe each
other? What if your employee or workmate is not doing things the way you
would prefer them done? Are you open to allowing them to be an individual? Are you open to differences, or do you just want them to conform?
What impact do these labels and assumptions have on their success? The
benefit of taking the time to reflect on how we label others and the potential impact it has on our workplace is brilliantly summed up by Rose in the
following thought:

> Perhaps one of your employees whose performance is suf-
> fering has been labelled as difficult to work with by her
> colleagues; but rather than fire her, you are able to identify
> the contexts that make her act out, helping her strengthen

her relationships, and drastically improve her performance and allowing you to discover a hidden gem in your department. (14)

Expectations and Judgement

When it comes to the concept of getting people to conform to our expectations and judgement, my thoughts immediately turn to family. After all, who else do we invest the most energy, hopes, and dreams in? I am the mother of four, a nana to three, a wife, a sister, a niece, an auntie, a daughter, and a friend. What about you? What roles do you play? With these many roles comes the inevitable need to try and guide, inspire, and support others. How we do this can often be both productive and detrimental. *Why?* Because just as the previous lessons in the book have shown us, we tend to lead, guide, and inspire the way we *think* the person needs to be led.

Impacting Others

Take some time to think about someone close to you who you want to inspire. Now think about how you are trying to do it. Sometimes the best way to reflect is put yourself in their shoes. If you were the one being guided, what would you need?

- When you think of people in your life, what role do you want them to play?
- Do you want them to tell you how to behave and perform?
- Do you prefer to set your own goals and expectations, and only seek advice when needed?
- How have you made your preferences known?
- Does the way someone guides you impact how well you learn?

Although the answers to these questions might seem easy at first, they are actually quite complex.

Learning the Hard Lessons

There are many hard lessons I have had to learn when it comes to guiding others, and most have come from family. I have given birth to two of my children, the other two were gifted to me through marriage. We are a truly blended family, with varying ages, goals, and aspirations. Each member has taught me a new lesson both in life and leadership. I have come to realize that what I want for someone is not necessarily what they want or need for themselves. I have realized, sometimes painfully, that I need to do more listening and less suggesting. They have taught me that I need to believe in them, I need to see them as individuals, I need to understand their interests, needs, and preferences, and I need to support them through their life choices. One of my favourite lessons came from my son Ryan when he was only about seven years old. We were about to attend a parent-teacher meeting. The teacher had asked the children to rate themselves on various behaviours prior to the meeting. It went something like this:

Under each word, please indicate how often you would say you display this behaviour:

Cooperation—RARELY, SOMETIMES, OFTEN, ALWAYS

Responsibility—RARELY, SOMETIMES, OFTEN, ALWAYS

Listen carefully—RARELY, SOMETIMES, OFTEN, ALWAYS

Participate in class—RARELY, SOMETIMES, OFTEN, ALWAYS

When it was our turn to sit down with the teacher, she reviewed Ryan's answers. Immediately she turned to Ryan and said, "Really, Ryan? You rated yourself as 'always responsible'?"

You see, Ryan didn't exactly fit the teacher's definition of an ideal student. He could be disruptive, energetic, loved to talk, and didn't love to read. For this teacher, the word "responsibility" was associated with being well-behaved and well-mannered in class. She would have rated Ryan very low on this scale. Of course, my anxiety piqued. No one wants their child labelled as a troublemaker in class. My expectations and goals for Ryan were to be an ideal student whom teachers liked and enjoyed in class. But instead of inserting my expectations and chewing Ryan out for ill

45

behaviour, I decided to take a deep breath and ask, "Ry, why did you put *always* in your rating?" His answer was a simple one, "Because I always take responsibility for the stuff I do wrong."

And there you have it. He was actually meeting my expectations when it came to honesty and integrity. I had always told him, "If you screw up, make sure I know about it before I get a call from the school." And he would. As just a little person, he would get off the bus and tell me, "I got a yellow card today. I had to stay in at lunch. I had to sit in the hall. I had to sit beside the teacher." He was being honest, took responsibility, and had paid the price. As we sat together on those little chairs at the parent-teacher meeting, I smiled. *Good for you, Ry. Good for you.* Needless to say, the teacher was not impressed. As a leader and a mentor, she had developed certain expectations of how her students should behave and rate their behaviours. Ryan was not fitting her mould. Neither did I. The fact that I had challenged her thought process and rating concepts meant I was not meeting her expectations of a supportive parent. Instead of siding with her, I had chosen to defend and support Ryan. With this came another common societal reaction. When things make us uncomfortable, we often label them as negative and less than. That's exactly what happened next. I was labelled as a *combative and confrontational* parent, and Ryan was labelled as an *irresponsible* child. But did it have to play out that way?

Labels We Use to Define Each Other

The subject of labelling and definitions of behaviour is one that I think we closely examine. *Why* do we have a need to label people? Why do we choose negative connotations for behaviours that make us uncomfortable? Why do we feel a need to rate and label people's behaviour, comparing them to what we deem as acceptable? What does this do to the people we are trying to lead and mentor? Does it help to build confidence and individuality, or does it minimize people into being less of their authentic self? These are really important issues for leaders to examine. There are many labels that we hear used the workplace: lazy, argumentative, not a team player, teacher's pet, golden child, etc. But what do these labels do to the people forced to wear them? Is our intent to shame, humiliate, and get them to conform to our accepted norms? *Why?*

How Have You Been Mislabelled?

We have all been mislabelled at times by others. Words have been used to describe us that don't seem to fit, or that cause us to feel devalued and disrespected. What are some of your labels? To really examine this concept, let's do a short exercise.

Take a few minutes and fill out this chart. Think about growing up, playing sports, school, and work experiences. Were there times that you were mislabelled?

Label	When/who used it?	How did it make you feel?

Think about the things that make **you** most proud to be who you are—your core values, your skills, your goals. Now what happens if people continuously tell you they are the wrong goals, poor skills, and misguided values? What if, as an individual, you are called out, made an example of, and labelled as *nonconforming*? How will you react? How does it impact you?

The Impact of Others' Opinions

People will have different reactions to being labelled. Some are able to shrug it off and rise above it. Others will find themselves making great efforts to try to disprove the labels and impress others. Finally, some will start to live out the label, behaving and acting in accordance with what society "expects" of them. It is vitally important to do some self-reflection and examine how you have reacted to your labels. Did they impact your own behaviours, choices, and expectations of others? It turns out, mine did. Again, one of my key life lessons came from parenting. This time it was my teenage daughter, Brianna, who would be my teacher. After a discussion on how I thought she should act in public, she shouted,

> Mom, STOP trying to tell me who to be. I am not like you. You worry about what people think too much. You try to be someone you're not—for your coworkers, with family, in life. STOP worrying about what people think of me. I don't care. I like being me. If people don't like it, well then, I don't need those people.

Wow, that was a showstopper. My heart dropped. Was she right? Was my need to try and please others and meet their unreasonable expectations also crossing over into my expectations for others? It was done out of love. I didn't want them to be subjected to the ridicule and cruelty of others' words and gossip about them. However, by doing this, I was asking them to tame or change who they were as individuals instead of celebrating and supporting their individuality. At work, I am often referred to by younger employees as their "work mom." Probably because they know I have grown to love them and support them the same way I would my family. I have hopes and dreams for them as employees and want to help them excel in their careers. I worry about how they are seen and viewed by others. But what if they don't want to meet these same goals, or perform the way I expect them to? Am I at risk of doing the same thing to them? As leaders, do we risk not only labelling employees but also smothering them from being their authentic self?

Labels Don't Disappear

In a workplace, employees are often "labelled" by their first coach, their first supervisor, on their first performance evaluation. We use terms like "she's a go-getter, he's a quick learner" to describe employees we are impressed with and feel will do well in the organization. However, we are also very quick to judge others as "really quiet, seems frazzled, a bit of a train wreck!" This label or description can literally *follow* this employee for the rest of their career, even if they work very hard to move beyond these initial definitions of *who* they are. New supervisors, colleagues, and coaches will say, "Oh yeah, I heard they are really disorganized and lack confidence." How do you think this impacts the person's ability to feel they are a contributing part of the team? By labelling others, do we risk demoralizing and shaming them? How does this impact their desire to perform or even stay with the organization? I have met many employees who let these types of negative labels impact their own self confidence and belief in their own abilities.

It is also equally important that we don't put too heavy an expectation on those we initially label as a "rock star." I am sure you can think of an employee you thought was "perfect, a highflyer," and then they seemed to fall from grace. What happened? Often it was due to the fact we, as leaders, placed them on a pedestal and in roles they weren't ready for, gave them too much freedom, and failed to guide them. Trying to meet the expectations that come with overly positive labels also impedes people. We expect perfection and forget they too have weaknesses and need to be led.

Breaking Down Labels

One of the key roles we play as effective leaders is helping to break down these labels. We need to find the value in each and every one of our members. We need to move beyond initial impressions and truly learn who they are. This is an essential role if we are to retain and empower our employees and build our organizations into the high functioning teams we need them to be. We need each member to bring their authentic self to work. We need to caution ourselves and others from labelling behaviours that we define as different and potentially uncomfortable. We need to ensure everyone is allowed to be themselves and challenge the use of assumptions and labels. Additionally, if we find that people are starting to "live their label," either through negative behaviour or by disengaging completely, we need to have the courage to talk to them about it. It is our job as leaders to inspire people. We need to highlight their strengths and unique qualities and remind them (just as Brianna reminded me) that they are special and valuable and *are not defined* by a label.

LESSON 6

Maybe It's ME Not THEM

I Can't Coach THEM!

Have you ever found yourself asking this very question? *What were they thinking? Why did they hire them?????*

As someone who has developed and facilitated a lot of courses for coaches and trainers, I have heard this complaint over and over. Within the first half hour of the course, participants would be sharing "war stories" about those terrible employees that "they" hired. The ones that couldn't get through training and ended up always in trouble. The ones that no one liked, and no one wanted to coach.

I would try to lighten the mood and show them that often an effective coach can make all the difference in someone succeeding or failing. I would include lots of self-assessments so participants could learn more about themselves and their coaching styles. We would discuss hypothetical coaching scenarios and concepts, and we would work through potential challenges they may have when training a new person. We used our PI assessments to learn more about the coaches and did multiple intelligence quizzes to see how they preferred to learn and potentially to coach. We talked about how they would need to meet the needs and learning styles of their trainees, and people generally left feeling a little more enlightened and excited to try out their new skills. As the months passed, I would watch as they fell back into their default behaviours and coach styles. I would hear all the grumbling and complaining about how new employees couldn't learn, they can't be trained, they are problem children. And so it began ...

Recruitment and Hiring Processes

As part of Human Resources (HR), I know how much effort organizations put into screening, testing, interviewing, and doing reference checks. When the successful candidate is finally called and offered the position, you are confident you have found the right employee for the job. Typically, the employee is then put through an onboarding process that introduces them to the mission, vision, and values of the organization. HR will cover all the necessary policies and procedures and ensure employee understand their job description and how they fit into the organizational chart. The employee may even write a short biography to share a few personal details about themselves with their new supervisor. Hopefully they are assigned to a coach or trainer. They may even have a training plan designed to set expectations and timelines for learning the new job. Off they go into the abyss, and you pray everything goes well.

Sadly, every HR leader reading this book knows what may come next. Most coaching scenarios present challenges and unique issues that will need to be resolved. Often it starts with the dreaded phone call from the supervisor or coach. *I don't know what you were thinking, but this person won't make it. What's wrong with your hiring process? We can't train them!*

Common Concerns

Sometimes the concerns present themselves after only a couple of weeks, or sometimes a few months later. The themes are usually the same:

1. The employee asks too many questions and thinks they know it all.
2. They just say yes when asked if they understand, but clearly, they *don't*.
3. They can't multi-task; they are too slow.
4. They can't keep up to all the changes and are already complaining.

5. They booked off sick already!
6. They can't seem to remember how to do something the way it was demonstrated. They don't follow all the steps.
7. They can't problem solve. They can't think for themselves.
8. Either they go, or the coach will.
9. They aren't going to make it.

And an HR favourite ... *YOU hired us the wrong person. What's wrong with YOUR hiring process?*

Everyone is stressed, and the inevitable cycle of blame begins:

- Supervisors complain that their new trainees are not making it and their staff is overworked and lacks the needed resources.

- People turn to HR and ask: *What's wrong with your hiring processes? What did you miss? Why can't they learn?*

- HR, feeling equally frustrated with the idea of having to start the whole process over, asks: *What's wrong with the trainers? The employee is a good one. We can't hire you anyone else!*

- The coach, feeling overworked and exasperated, says: *That's it, I quit. I am not coaching anymore people.*

- The poor trainee, feeling equally disillusioned and let down by the organization, ends up in HR inevitably in tears, lacking self-confidence, and fearing they are about to lose the job they worked so desperately to attain. They express their feelings of frustration and their lack of connection with the coach. They complain they can't learn from them and that they keep getting new opinions from new people who are trying to help. *Everyone has their own way they want me to do it. I am so confused.*

Does any of this sound familiar to you? If not, go and ask HR—I bet they have some similar stories to share. Why? Because for years we have all done it the same way, we were all trained the same way, and we are all missing a key link.

How Do You Coach and *Why*?

Let's go back to the beginning and examine how we train coaches. In some cases, trainers are just assigned by a supervisor to step up and "show the new guy the ropes." There is no formal training given to the trainer/coach on how to approach this teaching experience. They are likely just given a list of tasks, policies, and procedures and told to ensure the "new person" learns them. But do you actually teach them *how* to coach someone? Think back to the hockey analogy at the beginning of this book. The best coaches learn not only how to teach the skills, but how to *engage* the player, make them feel valued, and play off their strengths. They also coach their coaches to become greater. They work with the team and the coach to figure out what is working and what isn't. They watch from the bleachers and then come down to the ice to offer guidance and support. That is exactly what I want to do for you. So join me on the bleachers and let's watch a playback of what has been happening in our organizations and figure out how we can enhance these coaching relationships.

Learning More about the Trainee

First, we need to learn more about our trainees. My survey results further enhanced this point. When asked—**Does your supervisor/ coach try to adapt their training style to meet your preferred learning style?**—employees' responses clearly indicate a need for coaches to understand *who* they are coaching and how they learn.

Learning Styles

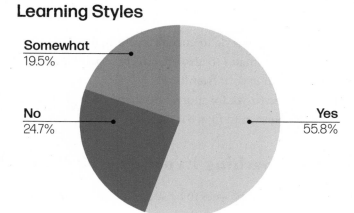

Somewhat
19.5%

No
24.7%

Yes
55.8%

YES

- Very open communication, provides emails with instructions when requested
- Helps in a way that is most beneficial to learning
- Allows email questions so responses can be saved for later
- Tries in order to get a task done
- Provides one-on-one coaching
- Teaches how to have courageous conversations, offers suggestions
- Sometimes focuses too much on teaching style and not enough on content
- Meets preferred learning style

NO

- Very rigid
- Not open to change or other methods
- Very autocratic and inflexible
- Does it their way only
- Talks about it but doesn't do it
- Prefers not to do it in writing so there's an "out" later on
- Feels threatened by questions, as if credibility is being questioned
- Other learning styles never discussed or considered

SOMEWHAT

- Tries
- Must adapt personal style to coach's teaching method
- Must rely on teammates to also effectively explain it a different way
- Only if the coach is your friend
- Sometimes need to ask for more, and then coach gets curious
- Typically left on own to figure it out

Starting the Coaching Experience off Right

All of us want our new employees to be successful. We want to build capacity, prevent burnout, and increase both skills and retention. To do this, first we need to set our coaches and trainees up for success.

One method is to introduce some new assessment tools into your coaching courses. In mine, I would ask coaches and trainees to first take a couple of minutes and complete a Multiple Intelligences (MI) quiz to determine their preferred learning styles.[5]

What Are Your Preferred Learning Styles?

- You like to have a visual diagram or draw things out = VISUAL LEARNER
- You want to study the instructions on your own and research how to do it without the assistance of others = INTRAPERSONAL LEARNER
- You like to participate in discussions and group exercises = INTERPERSONAL LEARNER
- You want to physically try it and learn to do by doing = BODY KINETIC LEARNER

---

5   I have included a link for a MI quiz on my website www. Inspiringorganizationalgrowth.ca for you to utilize. The results will help you better assess how you learn. Most people will find they have at least two preferred or combined learning styles.

- You enjoy listening to music while you learn/study. You create little jingles or rhymes in your head to remember things = MUSICAL LEARNER
- You need things to be in a logical and systematic order to learn them = LOGICAL/MATHEMATICAL LEARNER
- You learn best if you are outside in nature or near a window = NATURALIST LEARNER
- You like to listen to someone else talk and lecture and absorb the information= VERBAL/LINGUISTIC LEARNER

I am a *visual* and *interpersonal* learner. I learn best if someone draws me a chart or visually shows me how the project is supposed to look. I can't just sit in a lecture hall and listen to a professor talk. I will fall asleep. I learn best when I can discuss it with someone (my need to ask *why*), but not when they just show me how to do something. I am not a musical or a verbal learner. I have to have silence; music is distracting. I am not strong in mathematical skills or learning other languages.

Of course, the way you learn will also tend to be your preferred way to teach, coach, supervise, and parent. But what if the other person doesn't have the same preferences? As previously mentioned, some of my best life lessons came from my children. When I started to facilitate and use MI as part of my teaching, I also found child-appropriate examples for my children to complete. There are many examples on the Internet, depending on the age of the child you want to assess. They are fairly simple and lack complexity, but they still provided me with some much-needed insight into my own kids.

One such test was composed of questions similar to this:

1. When you hear the word *cat,* what first pops into your mind?

    - Do you see a cat? (visual)
    - Do you hear a cat? (meow)
    - Do you picture the letters C-A-T? (verbal)

2. If given the choice to do anything you want, would you:

    - Listen to music (musical)

- Kick a ball (body kinetic)
- Read a book (intrapersonal)
- Talk with a friend (interpersonal)

Ryan, my active, never-sit-still kind of kid, had always hated doing his homework—and so did I. We would take hours to just complete one assignment or read a book as we sat together on the couch. I was constantly telling him to stop fidgeting, sit still, pay attention, and *focus*. Instead of listening, he would be upside down on the couch, kicking a ball in the kitchen, and fidgeting with a toy. However, he would yell back, "I am listening, Mom!" And on and on it went. Until I had him do his own MI. Suddenly it all started to make sense. He was a body kinetic learner. Fidgeting, moving, kicking the ball was how he engaged his mind, and it helped him process. The minute I asked him to stop moving, he stopped learning. He was *not* an intrapersonal learner; he hated reading and trying to follow written instructions (we later learned he had dyslexia), but in the early years, we just had to adjust to his learning style. Instead of making him read the book, I read it to him. I would read the assignment to him, and suddenly as he was kicking the ball in the kitchen, we would be discussing the meaning of the book and what the character learned in the story. If given the choice to do a written story or create a video for an assignment, he always picked the latter. He'd go outside with his sister, the videographer, to create an interactive video that depicted the meaning of the book or assignment. Was he learning it the way I would have? No. Did it matter? Absolutely not. This continued into his high school years and beyond. He always had music going or a video playing in the background as he studied. It drove me crazy, but I wasn't the one learning. He listens to podcasts while he drives and cranks his music. He doesn't read books or instructions, but he will have great discussions and debates about what he has learned and fidget with something until he can figure out how to fix it. He is an excellent team player and loves to take on new challenges. Will he be everyone's ideal employee? He certainly can be. But ultimately it may come down to *who* are the coaches and leaders, how willing they are to potentially challenge themselves to work with someone who may be different than them, and what they learn about him *first* so they can properly mentor and guide him.

Sharing Our Behavioural Profile with Those We Lead

Think back to Lesson 3. If you were to take your PI assessment and share it with those you lead, what would they learn about you?

Now expand these thoughts to:

- What if you had their PI assessment (rather than the standard bio done in onboarding)?
- What could you learn about them? Would some of the results surprise you?
- How comfortable would you be in the differences that appear between you and them?
- How could a coach or trainer then also use this information to benefit them in their teaching style?
- Do elements of the PI and MI quiz blend together and start to give you even more insight into the person you are leading or working with?

Blending Your Profile and Your Learning Styles

I started to do a social experiment with the PI assessments and MI quizzes. In each of my next coaching courses, I had people complete their own assessments. Then we talked about them and how this knowledge would apply to their own leadership of others. In typical fashion, they left filled with new knowledge and theoretical application ideas.

Then the real work began. I would meet with a coach and trainee who had just done their own assessment. Usually, it was after they had been working together for a short period of time. They would be nervously smiling at each other. It was like they had an inside joke that I wasn't yet a part of.

"So what did you think of the assessment?" I would ask, and inevitably they would start to laugh.

In one instance, Scott, a coach, explained, "Well, it definitely explains a lot. We have been butting heads trying to figure out how to ensure that Jacob learned the needed skills. I would tell him how to do a task. I would take the lead and demonstrate it and then ask if he had any questions. He would just nod and say nothing. Then we would start the task, and he looked lost. It was like he had retained nothing. I would get frustrated and show him again. I wanted him to ask questions, talk it out, but nothing. He would just look at me."

Scott had been trying to institute coaching techniques he had learned in the coaching course and from his own initial coach:

1. Explain the task and its purpose
2. Demonstrate the task
3. Let the trainee complete the task
4. Provide feedback and discuss improvements

When he had been trained, he and his coach would have long discussions about their roles and talked about how Scott could improve. He incorrectly assumed that his new trainee would want to learn the same way, but it wasn't working. Luckily, we were able to meet early enough in the training that I could provide both coach and trainee with a better understanding of each other.

Example:

Scott was a **Promoter**.[6] He was social by nature. He loved to interact and discuss things with other people. When it came to his learning style, he was interpersonal and collaborative. He liked to talk it out. His trainee, however, was on the opposite end of the scale. Jacob was an **Analyzer**. He was much more reserved and preferred an intrapersonal style of learning. The idea of having to ask questions and discuss the task without first having had time to self-reflect and collect his thoughts was terrifying. In fact, if given the choice, he would have preferred to email his questions and receive written guidance that he could then review and research on his own.

Hearing this, some of you may be thinking, *Are you kidding me? You want me to type out responses to his questions and let him* think *about his answers?*

---

6   A PDF describing all 17 personality types/profiles can be found on my website under book resources. www.inspiringorganizationalgrowth.ca

This is ridiculous. I don't have time for that. I need him to learn it, demo it, and move on. We have lots for him to learn. He needs to adjust and overcome his fears. These are fair concerns and ones that have been vocalized to me when I bring up this example during a training course. But before we just say "no," let's take some time to examine *why* you are saying no, and what impact it will have on your team and your organization.

Developing Your Players

Let's again think back to the hockey analogy. For a team to be effective, you need to have defence players, offence players, and a goalie. On each line, you have two defence, two forwards, and a centre. You have at least two lines, so that makes four players filling each of the same roles. Now stop and think for a moment about the players who fill those positions. Does each carry out their role the same way? Does each one learn the game the same way and have all the same skills? No! In fact, in the early years of a player's hockey career, a good coach uses their differences in personality and in playing style to the team's advantage. Sometimes the coach will intentionally pair a very protective, assertive defence player with one who is a little more risk averse or timid. The assertive player may tend to lead most of the plays around the net and may start coaching the other player where to be and when to look for the puck. In comparison, the more reserved player also serves a key role. They tend to calm the more excitable assertive player, encouraging them to stay back, watch the play as it transpires, and plan ahead for their next defensive move. These players learn to adjust their playing styles and behaviours not only to each other, but also to that of the rest of the team. They don't try to become mirrors of one another; instead, they learn how to bring out the best in each other and use it to the team's advantage.

Still not convinced that you have the time to push yourself to coach and lead each person differently in accordance with their needs and interests? That's okay. Just promise me you will stay curious and continue to turn the pages of this book. I have some more links to show you that will help to demonstrate *why* getting to know *who* you are leading will make your job easier and improve your team's success.

LESSON 7

Don't Hire a Mini-Me
Who Do You Want to Hire?

We have all heard the adage "Employees don't quit their job; they quit their leader." In fact, my survey on effective leadership confirmed it with 74% of respondents indicating they have left or considered leaving an organization because of supervision. So let's take some time to really explore this concept and what it means for us as leaders and for our organizations. We all know that people will come and go from an organization. In fact, current data tells us that the average employee will have ten to twelve jobs in their lifetime (Lahey 2020, 18). There have been many books and podcasts produced to try and explain the various reasons for this. What do you think the reason is?

a. Millennials and Generations X, Y, Z. They won't commit to anything. They are focused on the next best thing.

b. Lack of opportunity for promotion. They realize quickly they will be stuck doing the same job for a long time.

c. They would have stayed, but they couldn't stand the boss.

d. They were frustrated with how things are run. They had great ideas and suggestions, but no one would listen.

e. They have more choices and opportunities than any other generation has had previously.

I think there is value and truth in each of these responses. I also know as a human resources professional we rarely take the time to ask people *why* they are leaving, and if we do, many people do not feel safe enough to tell us for fear of being judged and ridiculed when they leave. Ever heard the advice "apply for jobs while you have a job"? I think this stems from the same type of fear. Don't let anyone know you are unhappy. Apply for another job, get a good reference, and leave on good terms.

Let's be honest. Do we as leaders really want to hear what we did wrong or how it could be improved? Not really. Why? Because it would require us to hold up a mirror and acknowledge we may have been part of the problem. That's a tough ask. It could cause us to feel ashamed, embarrassed, and vulnerable. It is much easier to just let the person leave, blame it on their need to "find something new," and move on to hiring the next person. But *who* do you want HR to hire for you now? Do you feel that if the person was more similar, fit the job mould, and wasn't so challenging or independent, it would have worked out better? Do you instinctively know what kind of employee will fit in with your group better than another?

After all, you have been managing for years, you have seen employees come and go, you know who works well in your unit and who doesn't. You know the job inside out and what it takes to be skilled in it. So just hire that type of person, right? But there are a few other things coming into play that we need to examine. Remember, I gave the disclaimer at the beginning that this book was not for the faint of heart. So let's approach this a slightly different way and see what we uncover.

Who's Your Ideal Candidate?

What type of person do you think would fit the mould for your ideal candidate? When you think of your ideal candidate, think about the people you enjoy working with the most. Are you thinking entirely about skills and experience, or are you also focusing on personality and behaviours? In order to really explore this concept, I have designed a few questions for you to respond to. In answering, go with your first instinct, your gut, not the politically correct answer or the one you think you should select.

After each response, take a few moments to ponder:

- Why did you select that response?
- Were you thinking about a particular positive or negative experience?
- Were you thinking of a particular employee?
- Would you want to work with them again?

If you find it difficult to answer a question, think about why. What were you taking into consideration?

Who Do You *Like* to Work With?

1. Do you enjoy working with people of the same gender or gender identity as yourself?
   a. Yes
   b. No, I would rather work with those of the opposite gender
   c. Either is fine

2. When you are in a group setting, do you prefer people who:
   a. Listen and don't really speak up
   b. Share relevant details
   c. Share personal/random information
   d. Discuss issues and ask questions

3. Which people do you *dislike* the most in the same setting? People who:
   a. Listen and don't really speak up
   b. Share relevant details
   c. Share personal/random information
   d. Discuss issues and ask question

4. What is your immediate reaction when someone asks you about a decision you have made?
   a. I feel a need to defend my decision
   b. I am curious to hear their insight
   c. It depends on who is asking the question

5. Do you enjoy working with people who offer suggestions on your leadership style?

    a. Yes, I ask for that input

    b. No, keep your opinions to yourself

    c. It depends how they deliver the message

6. What type of people do you enjoy leading?

    a. Those who listen to your suggestions and follow them

    b. Those who listen to your suggestions and ask clarifying questions

    c. Those who challenge your ideas and have ideas of their own

7. Do you enjoy working with people who share their personal weaknesses and fears?

    a. No, save that for friends

    b. Only if it's not something I actually have to address

    c. Yes, I want to learn about how to help them

8. Do you prefer to hire a candidate who has already done the job and can immediately step into the position, or one you need to mentor and coach?

    a. I prefer someone who knows the job so we can keep producing

    b. I like to mentor and mould

    c. I want them to have some skills, but not too much experience

9. How do you prefer your employees to communicate with you?

    a. Send me an email

    b. Just come in and ask

    c. Book an appointment

10. When working in an office or a job setting, do you prefer people to:

    a. Work independently

    b. Work together as a group

    c. Work alone and then come together to review at the end

Do you think the way you have answered these questions might potentially impact *who* you select to promote or mentor for new positions?

Are We Ready for Different?

I wonder how you are reacting to this lesson. If we were in a classroom, I would be watching for body language. Things like crossed arms or eye rolling, which would indicate you are getting annoyed with these questions. Since you are reading this book, I need you to take a few moments and reflect on this question. Are you getting annoyed? Do you think it is ridiculous that I am proposing *you* might be part of the issue? That how you answered each question might lend to how you select employees?

Be honest, and now think about these points:

- Do you want your next manager, supervisor, or employee to be a carbon copy of the last? Why or why not?
- What were the strengths and challenges they brought to the position?
- What would you be looking for next time?
- Are you perhaps thinking about elements you selected in the previous questions?
- Can you work with someone who doesn't fit your selections?

What's Stopping You?

If you aren't ready for a change, what's stopping you? Some of my best leadership learning moments have come from people telling me I sucked. They were different from me, thought differently than I did, and didn't like my style. Not the easiest thing to hear. They criticized my approach, the way I handled a situation, the way I made them feel, or the lack of detail I applied to a matter. Of course, my immediate reaction was one of shame and embarrassment. I wanted to defend my practices and my decisions. And sometimes I did just that. What I really needed to do was get curious and listen. What I should have said was "tell me more." What stopped me was my ego. In his book *Ego Is the Enemy,* Ryan Holiday explains, "We can't work with other people if we've put up walls. We can't improve the world if we don't understand it or ourselves. We can't take or receive feedback if we are incapable of or uninterested in hearing from outside sources" (4). My need to feel in control and respected impacted my ability to hear the feedback and remain open to it. My internal voices were adding to this inability to hear. They were telling me, *You are trying so hard. Who are they to criticize you?* However, what I really needed to do was listen to how the message was being delivered. Was it a message of love—were they really just trying to help me? Was it a message of pain—were they trying to show me how I hadn't met their needs? As long as the message was being delivered in a respectful manner (not condescending and rude), then I owed it to them to listen. If it was initially being delivered in a rude way, then I needed to share how that made me feel, and how it hampered my ability to listen and learn. I also needed to consider my own biases that might be getting in the way of learning the lesson they were trying to teach me.

A Learning Opportunity

One of the key lessons I have learned is that the people who challenged me the most were the ones I initially considered most *different* from myself. They were also my best teachers. For example, I struggle with people whom I define as loud and intimidating. They demand that I put their interests first and will shout to be heard. Sometimes I don't know how to react to this. Growing up, I had learned to always put others first. One of my most vivid memories from my childhood taught me a lesson I have instilled as a core value. I was maybe five or six years old. A friend had given me a handful of pennies. I proudly showed them to my dad. He told me to give them back, saying, "you don't take things from other people; you earn them on your own."' So I gave them back. From that point forward, I didn't like to take things. If someone offered me a piece of cake or a candy, my automatic response was "no, thank you," even if I desperately wanted it. I can remember sometimes shocking myself with my response. It was so automatic. "No, thank you." What evolved from this was twofold. I always wanted to do for others, give gifts, put them first. I also had a very strong dislike for people who put themselves first. I couldn't understand it. I saw it as arrogance. The analogy "the squeaky wheel gets the grease" seemed to apply to them. The louder they yelled, the more they got. It was infuriating. But my frustration was really sourced from my own issues, my own story, not theirs. It took *years* for me to realize this. One of my best learning moments came from a teacher by the name of Anna Barsanti. She gave me a simple phrase that would change the way I tried to approach this and many other situations: "What I see in you I see in myself." Think about that for a minute. For me it means that the things that I see as good in others are things I admire in myself. The things that I interpret as bad in others are things I don't like about myself. The times in my life when I have taken from others I don't consider as proud moments. Instead, I admire the times when I have given to the point of exhaustion. Hence, I struggle with people who I interpreted as taking. Maybe, instead, I need to take time to learn the lessons they were trying to teach me. This would tie into yet another one of Anna's lessons, when she would remind me of the importance of being kind to yourself. After all, can we even serve others if we have not first taken care of ourselves? So perhaps the real lesson I was supposed to learn was this: People I previously saw as needy or annoying were there to remind me of the need for self care. They were not being selfish. They were instead teaching me that sometimes it is ok to put yourself first, especially if you want to be able to continue to serve others. [7]

Isn't that an interesting concept? So now, let's go back to the idea of who we want to hire. In my case, I would prefer to hire people who are externally focused on meeting the needs of others rather than internally focused on meeting their own needs. What does that then do for a team that I am leading? It may result in a group of people that literally exhaust themselves trying to meet the needs of others. A group that will continue to give and give, sometimes at the expense of their own needs. This is actually a very typical trait for people drawn to HR. They are givers. They put their heart and effort into focusing on the wellbeing of others. But is it beneficial or detrimental to an organization? After all, a career is supposed to be a marathon and not a race. If we all go at a 150% all of the time, rushing to change priorities and meet the needs of others, what might the result be? Maybe what I should consider is the insertion of a few people on my team who are more vocal and who stand up for their (our) needs. Maybe that would motivate everyone to slow down, focus a little more on self-care,

---

[7]   Anna Barsanti and I co-facilitated Inclusion Awareness Training courses in 2011. She continues to be an important mentor in my life.

and ensure that we all remain healthy. It's an interesting concept but a *really* hard one to execute. It would require me, their leader, to push beyond the boundaries of my own comfort and invite people in whom I first viewed as challenging. By doing so, the benefits it could offer to the team and organization are immense. Do you have any such learning moments in your life? Think about "what you see in others." What are the things you admire? What are the things you despise? Why? How does this then impact your leadership practices and the teams you create?

Trying Something New

So here is the challenge. The next time you are about to tell HR *who they need to hire,* take some time and honestly think about *why* you are setting the parameters you are. Is it more about your comfort than what is really needed in the job? Are you open to trying something new? Will you give that new person an honest chance? What does your team *need* in the next hire?

Believe me, the employee you do select will also be judging themselves very hard. Just like the kid that comes to a new school halfway through the year. They realize they are joining a pre-established team. They have heard everything about the person they are replacing, and that can be very intimidating. They very much will want to impress you and fit in. They will also need you to trust in their abilities and let them demonstrate just how they can make it work. Let them try. Different isn't always bad—it's just different. Remember the first time you watched your teen drive out of the driveway by themselves. Did they operate the vehicle the same way you would? Drive at the same speed? Drive with one hand or two? But they still got there. They have the skills. That's why you let them drive.

When we apply this concept to our hockey analogy, it brings up some very interesting points. Think of the coach or scout who is involved in draft picks. It's not only about picking a defence player or another forward. Are they also considering how this player will gel with the existing teammates? Yes, they are. In an article entitled "Hockey Scout: 5 Things They Always Look For," Vital Hockey Skills writer Jim Vitale tells us,

Hockey scouts are not just looking for skills, position discipline (knowing your role), size, shape, and critical thinking skills. A big deciding factor is *character*. In the example of Sidney Crosby, it is his character and attitude that dramatically impact his ability to inspire others on the team. He is both competitive, has a positive attitude, willing to work with others, and is eager to improve.

If you think of things from this perspective, does it broaden your ideas of *who* your team may need? Have you asked them? You might be surprised to hear that their idea of the next ideal employee differs slightly from your own!

In Lesson 8, we will explore how you can expand your potential scope, and aspects you are looking for in your next hire. We will discuss data-driven, objective ways to help you find the right fit for the job and for your team. We will also explore how utilizing this information can help you build trust and respect, even with candidates who turn out to be the wrong fit.

LESSON 8

Rely on Data

Finding the Right Fit

So how do we know if someone is suited for the job? If we can't rely only on instincts and our gut, what else can we use? We just learned in Lesson 7 that our own biases may be getting in the way of even considering someone different or new. But I don't want you to feel like you must just abandon all your expertise and experience. I want to introduce the PI Job Assessment tool that may help you gain some further insight. There are data-driven ways to get a better indication for who might best fit the job.

Job Fit Profiles

Over the years, I have had some great success using this tool to help new candidates better understand themselves and their potential job fit. First, we ask successful employees currently in the position to complete their own PI. Then we overlay all their assessments and create a foundational assessment for the job itself. It highlights the behaviours and traits of those in the job, and potentially why they are so successful in it. For example, think of a common role in most organizations. Payroll. This is a job that requires someone to be highly detail-oriented (none of us want them making errors on our paycheques). It is one that requires a strength in the ability to follow procedures, policies, structured rules, and processes. Often the work can be repetitive and steadfast. It requires the ability to audit and correct your own errors. Many payroll roles are filled by only one person, so they need to enjoy working independently and not have a strong desire for socializing and collaborating. I have met some absolutely fantastic people working in payroll. They are diligent and great at their jobs. But they aren't me. I couldn't do their job anymore than they would want to work in the fast-paced, ever-changing social atmosphere that I relish and love. By doing a job assessment (using payroll practitioners from across similar industries), you can create a baseline for what you are looking for in a payroll candidate. Of course, this is only one piece of the puzzle. You will still need to assess skills, experience, and knowledge for the given position. However, just knowing how to do the job doesn't necessarily mean a person is going to enjoy it or function well in it. The PI job profile assists people in learning more about what behaviours and traits go into the job, rather than just a job description that describes the roles and responsibilities.

Example:

Samantha's position as a radiologist is one that requires precision, attention to detail, and a steadfast appreciation for policies and procedures. There is no room for risk-taking or skipping of steps. As a supervisor, she was tasked with training Mike, who was interested in the role of medical transcriber in their unit. He had previous medical training and had worked in other settings in the hospital. Immediately, this caused Samantha concern. She knew that Mike had worked in other areas. She knew he was quite social, was not known for submitting detailed reports, and preferred to work in areas that required him to meet directly with patients and collect general health information from them. Samantha spoke to her manager about her concerns that Mike might not fit well into the transcription role. Instead of hearing her, the manager said, "Well, you said you needed someone, so I found someone! Now it is your turn to coach him." Needless to say, it didn't go well. The fact that Mike lacked the attention to detail needed to ensure there were no errors in the medical reports became quickly apparent. His work was sloppy and filled with errors. He didn't follow the policies step-by-step and often forgot to complete all of the required tasks. Both

Samantha and Mike were frustrated. Luckily, Samantha took some time to think about how she could explain the disconnect. She used this analogy.

Samantha: "Mike, would you try skydiving?"

Mike: "Yeah absolutely!"

Samantha: "Okay, me too. But I think the way you and I would approach it is completely different. I would take the lessons, read the policy manual, and check and recheck my equipment *before* jumping out of the plane. I think your approach might be a little more haphazard. You are more of a risk taker. You'd likely a brief overview of the process, strap on the parachute, and when the airplane door opened, you'd jump!

Mike laughed in agreement: "Yep! That sounds like me."

Samantha: "Okay, well, the issue we are having is that this job requires you to approach it the way I would with skydiving. Lots of rules, processes, procedures, and steps that must be followed. Unfortunately, you have been approaching it the way you would approach skydiving. Get the basic gist and jump right in. But just like skydiving, we can't afford for you to skip a step. It's life threatening. It has to be done the same safe way each time."

Mike thought about what Samantha had said. He finally understood that she hadn't been micromanaging him because she disliked him … she had been doing it to keep the patient safe by ensuring their tests were read correctly and nothing was missed. Although Mike enjoyed the medical field, he ultimately decided radiology was *not* the right area for him. He needed to find something that allowed a little more risk taking and flexible assignments. He ultimately decided to transfer out.

Does this sound familiar? Likely you already know the type of personality, behavioural traits, and interests that are not well suited to your area. Have you ever been forced to take on people that you *knew* were not going to be a good fit? Have you had people start with your unit, only to very quickly learn they hated the work, and they weren't happy? Did it result in frustrated coworkers, tired coaches, and an organization that may label your unit as one that never keeps anyone and therefore *must* have problems? If so, the PI job profile can help. It will allow you to objectively explain your needs to your manager *before* issues arise. You will be able to illustrate what your team needs and the personality profiles that are a good job fit. Your opinions will not be jeopardized by personal biases or preferences but instead are based on a data-driven analysis and are easily defendable.

When You Have to Say Goodbye

Having objective information can also help when you have to say goodbye. I have also used this strategy, similar to the way Samantha did, when meeting with someone who has not been successful in their job. No one likes to fail. No one wants to admit they can't do something or discover it's not what they thought it would be. Everyone wants to better understand the *why*. Why didn't I like it? Why could I not adapt? Tearful goodbyes have turned into hopeful conversations about their future as we sit and diagnose what went well, what didn't, and why.

 In fact, coaches and supervisors have also expressed that they felt better after they reviewed an unsuccessful trainee's PI profile against the job profile. Coaches can be equally embarrassed and frustrated when a trainee or employee wants to leave. Some will shrug it off, but others open themselves up to the questions: "Could I have done something differently? Why didn't this work? What do I do differently next time?" Others are also concerned about how this looks to the rest of the organization. They worry people will be asking, *What's wrong with them? They can't keep an employee for more than six months. They must be brutal to work for.*

Using the PI has helped all of us develop a better understanding of what is needed in an ideal candidate. It helps to explain the position using data that is objective and not personal or subject to bias. HR can even build some of these elements into pre-screening or interview questions to try and better tease out if the person will be a good fit. Candidates can be told from the outset that the position will require them "to like change and quickly adapt to new priorities" rather than just saying they have to multi-task. Emphasis can be put on the fact that a job requires the candidate to work on their own in an isolated office rather than just saying you need to work independently. In providing the candidate more insight into the behaviours required for the job, they will be able to do their own self-assessment, before they start, on whether they think the job will suit them or not.

Expecting Too Much of One Person

Finally, there are times when doing the assessments and comparing a person to the job at hand will help everyone come to the realization that they are asking for the impossible! In an era of downsizing and doing more with less, I have seen many examples of how we try to use the same employee to fill several *very* different roles. Sometimes the reason we can't find the ideal candidate is because they don't exist! One person can't be expected to excel at all things. They will need to ask for help and reach out to those who excel in different areas than they do. An example of this can often be found in small businesses.

My brother is a classic example. Since he was in his early twenties, he has been the owner/operator of a historical stone masonry company. He has grown the business from small chimney repairs to award-winning million-dollar jobs on historical landmarks. He does absolutely amazing restorative work on historic buildings, bringing them back to life and repairing the stone in such a way that you would never know he had even been there. My brother is a true body kinetic learner. He loves to work with his hands, is super creative, and is a great relationship builder. His crews love to work for him. They work hard and laugh a lot, all while knowing he wants a job well done and that he will work right alongside them to get the job done. Sounds perfect, right? True, except that running your own business also requires a lot of paperwork, estimates, billing, payroll, permits, etc. If my brother had to do it all alone, he would be in trouble. Not only is it too much for him to maintain all aspects of the business, but his behavioural profile would also show a lack of desire to excel in all areas. He needs a bookkeeper, an accountant, and his wife to help him stay on track with all his paperwork and payroll. He needs to rely on specific crew members who are more skilled in stone carving than he is to help him replicate some of the broken stones they need to repair. It takes a team to bring the business to life and maintain it.

Now take this concept and apply it to your own position. Are people expecting or demanding that you can do it all—even things that are not within your knowledge or strengths? This is often the cause of workplace tension and conflict. It is often presented to HR as *people are not living up to the expectations of their supervisor or manager*. It is presented as a performance issue that needs to be addressed. We are told to find the personal training courses that will assist them in learning the needed skills. The employee will be put on a performance review so that we can properly monitor their success. In many cases, this employee had been previously recognized and awarded for their skills. In fact, it was due to their success in other areas of the organization that they were granted this new position. Now the employee is mortified to learn that they are being put on a performance review. I have spent hours with employees whose trust in their organization diminishes further as they find themselves being called out for their errors and publicly humiliated for their lack of ability in the new area. No one, including the employee, can understand what's happening.

Job Assessments

Using a Job Assessment tool and the resulting job profile, supervisors can clearly outline the role requirements and complementary behaviours needed to excel in the role. This can be done prior to selecting someone for the role. In the case of PI, a candidate's own PI assessment can then be compared to the job profile. This prevents the biased assumption that because someone excelled in one area of the organization, they should be able to quickly adapt to a new set of skills and behaviours found in a new position.

Example:

Greg had been an excellent science teacher. He loved working with the students, developing new ways to teach the concepts of developing hypotheses and proving theories. Students enjoyed his dynamic classes, animated discussions, and wild experiments. His excellent work caught the attention of the principal, who recommended him for a sabbatical position to work on the development of a new science curriculum designed to measure students' increased math and problem-solving skills. At first, Greg was honoured to be offered the position, but his excitement was quickly replaced with fear and self-doubt. Only a month into the new position, Greg was falling behind, not meeting expectations, and feeling the pressure to perform. The position was so unlike anything he had ever done. He worked alone in an office. He had to research and develop reports that would serve as a board-wide curriculum for Grade 4 science classes the following fall. He had to ensure that each plan was measurable, met learning criteria, and was defendable. His immediate supervisor communicated only by email with no verbal interaction, and would send back reports highlighted in bold-red advising he didn't like the format of the reports, wanted more detail, needed more concrete concepts, and wanted Greg to ensure he had referenced all his research and examples. Greg was lost. Not only did he not know how to do the reports, but he also lacked the personal motivation even to work on the reports. He missed his students. He liked interacting with them and the other teachers. He loved to collaborate and learn to do by doing. *After all, wasn't that the fun of science? Experimentation?* When it came to trying to put these ideas and concepts into a detailed, defendable bureaucratic report, he felt like he was out of his league. He called his principal for some advice and insight. The two discussed the issues at hand and reviewed the PI assessment he had completed a few years earlier.

- Greg was interactive; he liked collaborating and working with others.
- Greg liked to think about the bigger picture—helping students develop a love for science.
- Greg was a risk taker—his lesson plans were always a little *off the cuff,* and he moulded them to the needs of the students.
- Greg loved to verbally interact and rarely put his thoughts into detailed written format.

No wonder this new position was not well suited to Greg! However, instead of quitting, he wanted to try to find a way to make it a success. Armed with these new realizations, he requested an in-person meeting with his new supervisor. He explained his strengths and preferred ways to behave

LESSON 8

and operate. He acknowledged the need for the project to have some of his skills, but also the need to involve someone else who was more detail-oriented and had the ability to work with him to move these ideas and concepts into the well-researched report his supervisor needed. It worked! They assigned another person to work with Greg who had a report-writing and research background. They set up Zoom meetings so that Greg and his new partner could collaborate with other science teachers to enhance the ideas and suggestions for the new lesson plans. In the fall, the new science format was ready, and Greg went back to the job he truly loved ... teaching science in the classroom.

In both examples, the utilization of data-driven information allowed Mike and Greg to maintain their self-esteem and build a sense of respect and trust between them and their supervisors. Although the outcomes may vary, the data found within a job profile and a person's own PI assessment provides access to needed information and will assist in the development of creative options for those struggling to accomplish job demands.

80

PART 3

—

DEVELOPING TRUST, REMOVING TRIGGERS, AND BUILDING TEAMS

LESSON 9

A One-Size-Fits-All Approach Doesn't Work

How Do We Rate Each Other?

When the email shows up telling you that it is time to complete your performance appraisal, your immediate reaction is (let's be honest ...):

a. Oh yeah! I have been waiting for this.

b. Are you ?!#% kidding me! What a complete waste of time. No one reads it.

c. I am going to be sick. I hate rating myself.

d. This is so unfair. They never rate people fairly. It's just a popularity contest.

As a human resources professional, I prided myself in knowing that performance evaluations and scales were objective and fair. HR professionals put a lot of effort into market research, ensuring the language we use is nonbiased, objective, and based on averages and expectations for the job groups. We ensure that everyone is rated utilizing the same matrix, and supervisors need to justify their rating and explain them. Everything needs to be transparent and fair.

This turned out to be another good hard life lesson. Although the theory behind the processes is sound, I quickly learned a one-size-fits-all approach doesn't work. When I met with the actual people regarding their performance appraisals, I discovered they were often utterly frustrated and very hurt. In his book *The End of Average*, Todd Rose states, "Our minds have a natural tendency to use one-dimensional scale to think about complex human traits such as intelligence, character, or talent. But one-dimensional thinking fails when applied to just about any individual quality that actually matters" (81). Now apply this to how we evaluate performance in organizations. HR training teaches us to develop standardized rating scales for performance in specific job groups. The purpose is to develop objective scales so that supervisors can rate an employee's performance against the expected and accepted norms for the position. However, often our attempt to make scales generic actually results in a scale that doesn't really suit anyone or allow their individual traits and talents to shine through.

It Doesn't Apply to My Job

Sometimes the criteria a person is being measured by does not even apply to the position. Let me give you a very basic example. Zack works on the production line at an online distribution company. He fills orders as they come in and sends them to shipping. He has very little autonomy in his role and has to follow strict protocols and timelines. He has been with the company for one year and has been asked to complete his first performance appraisal. As he looks at the first question, he is already frustrated and baffled.

1. Problem-Solving Skills

Please rate yourself on your ability to contribute to solving issues and problems that arise in your unit.

0 — I do not contribute to solving issues.

1 — I wait for direction from others.

2 — I provide limited insight into how to solve the issue.

3 — I often provide insight and suggestions on how to solve issues.

4 — I provide innovative and insightful solutions to solving problems.

How is he supposed to fill out this first rating scale? Should he give himself a zero out of four because he isn't in a role that even allows him to contribute to solving issues? Has anyone even asked him if he has ideas on how to improve the processes? Not likely. Does this mean Zack lacks problem-solving skills, or rather that he hasn't been given the opportunity to demonstrate them? Even more importantly, how does this rating system make Zack feel? Does it make him feel like he is contributing to the organization? The organization must value people who *provide innovative and insightful solutions to solving problems.* After all, people who can answer "yes" get four out of four, which equals a 100% on this competency. So now what? What does that mean in terms of Zack's value to the organization? How do we bring across his individual talents and qualities that add to the organization?

Other competencies and abilities found in his performance appraisal are:

Ability to Resolve Conflict. Again, Zack has to defer to his supervisor, so he will likely rate low on this scale. He will earn a one out of four rating.

1 — I will make my supervisor aware of any issues that arise.

Ability to Manage Risk. Zack is not involved in strategic risk aversion discussions. Again, he scores one out of a potential four points.

1 — I follow predetermined rules and protocols.

Leadership. Zack doesn't lead or coach anyone. This time he earns a zero.

0 — I do not provide leadership or guidance to others.

Relationship Building. Zack works independently to get his job done. He's not an overly social person, so he doesn't spend his breaks chatting with fellow employees; he just eats his lunch and listens to a podcast. That will equate to a one out of a potential four points.

1 — I am cordial with my fellow employees.

Assessing Personal Value

I think you get the idea. Overall, if Zack converts this to a percentage, he may be left with the impression that he only scores 25% as an employee.

In the book *First, Break All the Rules* from Gallup, we are introduced to the results of interviews conducted with more that a million employees over the last 25 years to determine satisfaction in the workplace. The survey, entitled "How to Measure the Strength of a Workplace," asked employees what are the core elements that are needed in an organization to attract, focus, and keep the most talented employees. They landed on 12 elements that need to exist within a workplace. As we move through this book, I will introduce you to many of these key elements.

However, in relation to the concept of performance measurement and how it may impact an employee's feeling of belonging and worth in a workplace, let's consider element four.

Element 4: In the last seven days, I have received recognition or praise for doing a good job.

This element is key to why employees remain or leave an organization. Keeping this in mind, you will recognize that Zack's overall sense of value and need within the organization is likely to be fairly low. This will be further reinforced if this appraisal is the first time this year (or even more) that his performance has even been addressed. Does his supervisor periodically meet with him and praise/thank him for work well done? Or is there a tendency for the supervisor to disregard Zack since he is such a good employee and doesn't need direct leadership or guidance?

Examine Your Own Performance Appraisals

With this concept in mind, grab one of your own business performance appraisals. Look at the competencies and ratings. Think about a role in your organization that is likely an entry-level position, or one that requires following strict guidelines and processes. Now picture someone who is very effective in that role and fill out your appraisal as if you were rating them. What kind of ratings are you giving them? Do you know how they feel about these ratings?

My own survey responses also give us further insight into this topic:

Does your supervisor/coach regularly provide you with feedback on your performance?

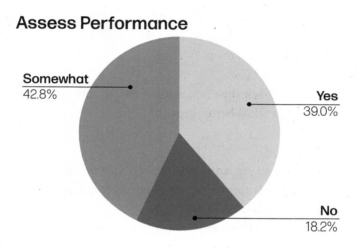

Assess Performance

YES

- Regular surprise visits to workspace and feedback on performance
- Shows appreciation
- Nature of job means regular feedback (weekly/bi-weekly)
- Regular meetings with feedback
- Asked for self assessment and then given feedback on goals
- Provides praise, support, and encouragement
- Constructive criticism when asked or needed

SOMEWHAT

- Occasionally, but often too busy
- Just in the beginning
- Sometimes given a backhanded comment that's meant to be positive, "who would have thought *you* could do that," but is not helpful

- A little more feedback would be appreciated in case I am off track
- When necessary, I find too much feedback insulting
- Rarely gives direct praise but tells other people about my good work
- Performance management is unequal. If I make a mistake, I get called out; if someone else makes a mistake, the boss expects me to fix it
- Only when asked for or absolutely necessary
- A lot of my job is to figure it out and only involve management when something is critical. Not always beneficial, but it makes me think critically on my own.
- Only on evaluations
- Sometimes feedback slips into a conversation, but more direct feedback would allow better growth

NO

- Only when criticizing; an excuse to withhold merit pay or raise
- Communication is something my supervisor needs to work on
- Nothing is ever good enough
- You hear of others' downfalls that never get addressed
- Supervisors fear not being politically correct so they don't give feedback
- Extremely rare
- Hasn't said anything to me in my first month—makes me feel unappreciated
- Sometimes it expresses their judgement of me—not productive
- Some of the performance measurement criteria don't even apply to me (interacting with people), so it is useless

I am introducing you to these concepts with the intent of making you rethink, re-examine, and challenge yourself on how and why we do things. Before you move further into this lesson, take some time to reread the comments above and consider your own leadership style and approaches. *(Remember, no one is asking you to share this personal insight, so be honest and vulnerable in your answers.)*

- Do you praise/thank employees for work well done?

- If so, how often?
- Do you tend to focus your attention or comments (negative and positive) on particular employees? Why?
- Do you think there are some employees under your leadership that may be feeling less valued?

How Can I Make Appraisals Relevant to *This* Employee?

Another issue that often emerges with performance appraisals is the supervisor's discomfort in completing them. Supervisors have told me they don't know how to make some employees fit into the boxes. They don't want to rate employees too high and risk offending others who are more average, but they also don't want anyone to feel bad. Looking back at the biases that we discussed in Lesson 4, many of these behaviours come into play when completing performance appraisals.

Recency Bias — The rating of someone's overall performance based solely on a recent event or interaction (Last week they did great.) (Yesterday they were late!)

Halo Bias — The rating of someone's overall performance based solely on one positive event or interaction (They did a great job on that one project.)

Horn Bias — The rating of someone's overall performance based solely on one negative event or interaction (They did so poorly on that one assignment.)

Similarity or Affinity Bias — The rating of someone's overall performance is biased or impacted by the rater's similarity to them (We went to the same school, have the same background, worked in the same unit.)

Contrast/Comparison Bias — The rating of someone's overall performance in contrast/comparison to another person (This employee is more effective at A than B; therefore, they should get a higher rating.)

Leniency Bias — The rating of someone's overall performance is better than it should be based on their performance indicators (I like them, they are a nice person, I didn't want to cause waves or upset them, so I rated them higher than I should have.)

Now think about when you have completed performance appraisals for your employees:

- Do you find yourself trying to increase the rating you are giving your ideal candidate due to one of these biases?
- Are you worried about how someone may feel if they only get one and two ratings?
- Do you find yourself trying to equate their value to a rating?
- Do you compare one employee to another when completing the ratings? (*If I give her a four, then he needs to get a three.*)

What if this employee is someone who comes to work every day, does their job, nothing more, nothing less, and leaves? Remember the old fable about the tortoise and the hare? The tortoise's approach was slow and focused on the race. He was quiet and reserved. The hare was tenacious and overconfident. The hare would be that employee who draws a lot of attention to themselves, is social, bounces around, and brags about their accomplishments. Which one do you favour? Which one might rate higher in your performance appraisal? In the end, does it even reflect who they are as employees?

Does One Out of Four Equal 25%?

If a rating scale is out of four, does a one equal 25% effort or success? I will be honest. Initially I did not really think it was a concern that someone got ones or twos. After all, that's the rating that fits. It didn't mean they were a poor employee in my mind. However, I soon learned this is exactly how it felt for employees. They were genuinely fearful of getting a low rating. "What if I only get a two? Does that mean I am only 50% successful? How do I describe and justify my ratings? What if my supervisor thinks I am being cocky and arrogant by giving myself a three?" I suddenly realized that there was a lot more going on here than rating performance. Employees who were otherwise stellar employees told me they were nauseous and anxious about meeting with their supervisor. Really? Why? They were excellent employees who gave 150% to everything they did. Why were they worried? Perhaps it was the concept that they were being compared against a set of organizational expectations of how they should behave and perform. They were worried about how they would be labelled and poorly rated by a supervisor who didn't like aspects of their personality or skills. One example sticks out in my mind. An employee was asked to rate themselves on their ability to resolve conflict. They gave themselves a one. I then rated them a two.

The discussion that followed was another great leadership lesson for me.

I started out in my normal fashion, trying to build up their confidence and explain in accordance to how I define conflict resolution that they did a great job. I explained that I knew them to be a very non-confrontational person. They didn't like conflict. So, in turn, they were very good at listening to people's needs and trying to find a compromised solution that would help address the person's unhappiness with a situation. I thought they did a great job.

When we looked at the competency and how it was rated, I felt they should receive a two.

Ability to Resolve Conflict:

1. I make my supervisor aware of any issues that arise.
2. I attempt to compromise and meet the needs of the person involved.
3. I actively discuss their concerns and address the conflict.
4. I mediate conflicts that arise and resolve issues.

Their reaction was one of sadness and defeat. I was shocked. I asked them to explain. What they told me has completely changed how I look at performance evaluations and their purpose. The discussion that followed provided me with further insight into who they were as a person and why they were conflict averse. Growing up, they had parents that fought, yelled, screamed, and argued. Their role as a child was to simply try to accommodate the needs of each parent, cook dinner, clean the house, and stay out of the way. If they knew a fight would be about who was going to clean up after the meal, they would simply be the first one to gather up the plates and wash the dishes. If they knew that their dad would want to put his feet up and have a beer after a hard day at work, they would meet him at the door with his beer and then help with dinner so their mom wouldn't feel overtaxed and taken advantage of. They found it best to simply not engage in arguments and in fact try to prevent them. If an argument did ensue, they fled to their room and listened to music until it was done. Now they feared that their inability to deal with conflict in the workplace would impact their ability to move up into a leadership/supervisor position. After all, to gain a 100% rating they needed to be able to *mediate conflict and resolve issues.*

Asking *Why* Helps You Gain More Insight

I had gained more insight and knowledge from asking *why* than I did from giving them a generic rating on a scale. My willingness to listen also helped to assure them that I didn't equate their two as failure. Even more importantly, I had managed to respond to two elements found in Gallup's *First, Break All the Rules:*

Element 11 — In the last six months, someone at work has talked to me about my progress.

Element 12 — This last year, I have had opportunities at work to learn and grow.

Suddenly I had goals to focus on with this employee. I now knew of their interest in succession planning and taking on a leadership role. I could introduce them to the fact that not all conflict resolution styles mean you need to get into the middle of the boxing ring and break up the fight. In fact, the type of interest-based mediation I am trained in is focused on making each party feel heard and valued. It ensures that the process is conducted in a very respectful way, absent of any yelling, blaming, or shaming. In the coming months, I would be able to model this for the employee and expose them to ways to play on their own strengths and in fact hit a four on that scale by *mediating conflict and resolving issues.*

How We Interpret Meaning

Another key component I have learned about evaluations is in our definitions. In the first part of this lesson, I intentionally didn't define conflict resolution or problem solving for you. I wanted you to think about your ratings based on your own interpretations of what those terms meant.

Think back to my example from Lesson 5. Ryan and his teacher had different definitions of the word *responsibility*. For his teacher, responsibility was associated with being well-behaved and well-mannered in class. She would have rated Ryan very low on this scale. Ryan had given himself a high rating, as he defined it as his ability to take responsibility for the stuff he did wrong. That conversation about the differing ways they interpret/define the word wouldn't have occurred unless I prompted the discussion to happen.

Now look back at your own performance appraisal.

- Does it provide definitions of the competencies it is trying to assess?
- Do you agree with the definitions?
- How will you determine if you and your employee agree on the definition?
- Are there opportunities to build in processes or discussions that will help you get to know the employee beyond their assessment?

In the coming lessons we will delve into a deeper look at assessments from both an organizational perspective as well as a cultural one. We will explore what we may be missing and *why*.

LESSON 10

Learning How You Impact Others

You Trigger Me

I discovered early on that when you conduct training for an entire organization, your classes become mini societies filled with power dynamics, learning preferences, and life stories you, as an instructor, are *not* aware of. I used to conduct courses for new employees, bringing everyone together for a couple of days to get to know each other better and hopefully help them to better connect to the organization and each other. It was one of my favourite courses to run. Each time I ran it, I learned new lessons about human interaction, past traumas, diversity, and how it impacts our workplace. So many of the lessons learned in that classroom forever impacted how I would conduct myself with individual employees, engage teams, and attempt to resolve conflict. The lessons I learned were valuable ones and can easily be transferred to your work environment.

Let's Start with How You Learn

When asked about how you learn, people will often share memories from their school experience. Luckily our school systems are starting to be more engaging and adapt to multiple learning styles. Think back to the classes that were most engaging compared to those that nearly put you to sleep.

What did you like? Interestingly, studies show that between 10–30% of the general population are strictly intrapersonal, verbal learners, and 70–90% of us will need other stimulation (visual, discussion, experiential learning). Despite this, many post secondary school systems are still based on listening to long lectures from in-class teachers or now, worse, on a virtual computer screen! I remember sitting in the lecture hall during my first year Intro to Psychology class and looking over my notes. You could see where I was writing, and then the pen would slowly side off the page as I fell asleep. Now think about those long meetings you have attended or the day-long organizational strategic planning sessions you've attended. Did they engage the learners by letting you move around, change tables, have discussions, or was it primarily PowerPoint lecture-based? The intent of these meetings is to generate new ideas, strategically examine how to move the organization forward, yet we never think to ask: *Who do we have in the room, and how do they need to be engaged?*

- Now, imagine if you did these same exercises in your team setting:
- What do each of your employees like and dislike about the work environment?
- Are there things that occur that negatively impact their learning?
- What can they do to support each other's learning?

Rules of Engagement

When I teach a course, I begin with the class setting the rules of engagement. My brilliant teacher and mentor, Anna Barsanti, taught me to ask my participants, "What are things that help you learn; what are things that impact your learning?"

What would you add to your list?

The class would make a list on a sheet of paper and then hand it in. I would tally the results and put them on a PowerPoint for all to read. It often looked like this:

Things That Help Me Learn	Things That Impede My Learning
Classroom discussion	Being asked to share my ideas in a group setting
People listening to the instructor	Cell phones ringing and people texting
Breaks every hour (coffee, cell phone, bathroom)	Long verbal lectures
Being able to read the material ahead of time	People swearing
Having an itinerary/syllabus	People interrupting and talking over each other
Getting up and moving around	Group activities
Sitting with people I know	Side conversations

Sharing the *Why*

Once the list was created, I would allow people who felt safe to do so to share *why* they had added certain items to the list so that the class could learn more. For example, you will see that some of the items, like the first one, *classroom discussion,* fall on both sides of the chart. Some people want to verbally engage with each other, while for others this literally causes them anxiety. In this case, those on the right side of the chart weren't about to verbally share their *why* with the class, so I did it for them. I spoke to the class about how participants sometimes approached me prior to the course expressing sheer dread! They had heard there were group exercises and activities, and because of this, they *really* didn't even want to even attend the course. Admittedly, the first few times I heard this reaction I had been a little taken back. As an instructor, I would quickly assure them it was a lot of fun, people enjoyed themselves, and it would be fine. Although I meant well, I was actually being extremely insensitive and did absolutely nothing to help people feel more reassured. This had been very important sharing they had done, and something I *needed* to take into consideration. After all, the course had been created to allow people to engage and get to know each other. How would we do that if they weren't even in the class or were filled with anxiety the whole time? I needed to design ways to increase their comfort. So we created a "pass system" that would allow those who didn't want to verbally participate to disengage and remain comfortable without having to provide a long explanation. They would just say "pass" and we would move on to the next person. By doing this and allowing them to ease into their comfort with the group, we would often find they did start to participate later. By sharing the fact that some participants' learning may be impacted by the fear of having to verbally participate, other members also learned valuable lessons. They were able to then take this learning outside of the classroom. Allyships formed, and often later in meeting settings, a more vocal or interpersonal person would offer to share the person's ideas during the discussion, putting that member more at ease and ensuring their thoughts were still heard.

Some of the other items on the list are a little easier to work through. For example, during meetings and training, you need to ensure you have breaks for people to engage with each other, answer cell phones, emails, and text so that they don't feel obligated to do so during the class. Having a syllabus or agenda is an easy addition so that your logical, detail-oriented, and risk-averse learners can understand the intent and process they are engaging in.

Our Past Impacts Us

Other items found on the right side of the chart were more deeply rooted. People's past experiences play a key role in how they want to engage with people moving forward. For example, many participants would share that they grew up with parents/family who were loud and verbally combative; therefore, they were triggered by yelling and swearing. When they heard it, they would mentally just shut down and disengage. Others shared that they had had partners and workmates who would talk over top of them and shut down their ideas before they were able to share them. All these personal details needed to be respected in our classroom if we were to create an environment of learning and respect. We started to understand how our behaviour choices impacted those around us. To enable effective learning, we needed to know what might *trigger* other people and how we could inadvertently impact someone else's ability to learn.

Discovering Triggers Activity

To discover what triggers might exist in your current group, you can try this simple exercise (it can easily be adapted to a virtual setting as well, but I will explain the in-class version so you have a visual of what it would look like). Ask each person in the room to write down on a paper a word, an action, a saying that *triggers* them. Then invite each person to put their paper in a bowl. The bowl is then passed around, and each participant pulls out a paper and reads what's on it. The author then has the opportunity to share more with the group about *why* they wrote the phrase or word, or they can pass and simply remain silent, allowing the class time to ponder the meaning. I have participated in this exercise many times. Some phrases are pretty apparent and don't need a lot of explanation: "stupid," "shut up," "that's so gay," are ones that come up in every class as phrases we should eliminate from our organizational language. They are viewed as dismissive and biased. Other phrases, however, are less apparent. I remember one such phrase: "brain dead." When read out, the author quietly spoke up to explain. In tears, they recounted that they had recently lost a close friend. The friend had suffered a fall and had been diagnosed as "brain dead." The friend had later passed away. Hearing the phrase shared as an insulting term among colleagues was triggering. They found themselves lost in memories and unable to concentrate on the task at hand. Everyone was silent. Then a teammate and colleague spoke up, saying, "I am so sorry. I use that term all the time. I had no idea. I won't say it again." This small acknowledgement of another person's needs and the willingness of a colleague to change their own behaviour went a long way towards helping these two teammates create a new sense of trust and dialogue.

Microaggressions

The trigger activity can also be very effective for introducing the group to the concept of *microaggressions*. *OxfordLanguages* describes microaggressions as utterances, statements, and actions that, while subtle and potentially indirect, impede the ability of a member of a marginalized group to feel included and accepted. Often terms people bring up as triggers are ones that can also be labelled as microaggressions. Admittedly, I have struggled to grasp this concept and have had to do a lot of personal reflection and seek out more insight to increase my understanding. I have learned that microaggressions can be very deeply rooted in our beliefs and actions. They may come from a place of privilege and biased assumptions. When challenged on our comments or actions, we may want to try and explain our intent and justify our actions. This is not the correct approach. In her podcast discussion "Creating Transformative Cultures," diversity, equity, and inclusion expert Aiko Bethea explained that "it's not about the intent of your comment, it is the impact it had on the person. You need to just sit with that and understand how you impacted someone else." Luckily, I have a diverse set of friends who have been willing to help me unpack this further. Friends with multicultural backgrounds have shared how they are *triggered* by phrases people use, such as "you are so well spoken." When invited to share further, they explain that it introduces the presumption that coming from a marginalized community, they would be poorly educated and lack professional diction. Additionally, these microaggressions can extend to other triggers, such as, "where are you really from?" This question is typically posed to people who are viewed as "non white." The speaker seems to assume that the person must have immigrated to Canada. Think about how this may impact the receiver. It may leave them feeling a need to once again have to justify or rationalize their history, their story. How often does this occur? How tiring and devaluing it must be.

Other examples of microaggressions have also been shared by members of other marginalized groups. Several of my friends from the transgender community have shared how phrases like "So what's your real name?" or "Have you fully transitioned?" can be soul crushing. The impact of this question, regardless of its intent, is enormous on someone who is simply trying to live their authentic self and be accepted by others for who they truly are.

As leaders, we need to be willing to learn and be accountable for our mistakes. If someone has the courage to tell you that your comment was a microaggression, thank them for their honesty. Don't make excuses or try to explain your intent. Regardless of what your intention was, the importance lies in the *impact* it had on the listener. I would like to thank those who have pointed out to me my own missteps and errors. The messages were at times very hard to hear, but the lessons behind them are invaluable.

The Impact of Your Efforts

Taking the time to learn how you are impacting and potentially triggering others can dramatically increase your ability to create an inclusive and diverse workplace. Introducing tools like the trigger activity should, in my opinion, be something that all leaders, supervisors, team coaches, and mentors use to develop trust and respect within organizations. I have personally watched as teammates, employees, and friends become much more conscious of what they say after participating in this activity. Additionally, they recognize that if they make blunders, they need to acknowledge them right away so as not to offend or hurt the other person. Teams also become protective of each other and will "police" others to ensure words, phrases, and terms are not used in their presence. An example of this is the Spread the Word campaign initiated in 2011 by the Special Olympics Foundation, designed to encourage people to stop using the word *retarded*. Sadly, the phrase has become vastly popular due to movies and social media. Exercises like the trigger activity often help to shed a light on why campaigns such as this are very important to people, and why misusing the R-word can be not only offensive but hurtful to people with intellectual disabilities. Members in sessions would often share how misuse of the term made them uncomfortable to share aspects of their personal life, including the fact they have family members or children with intellectual disabilities. Teammates, hearing this, immediately recognized the importance of eliminating the phrase. To ensure the learning became practice, some teams chose to use methods of having people quickly pipe up with a replacement word, like *ridiculous*, anytime the R-word was accidentally used. Other offices created a *trigger jar* in which people had to contribute money to charity if they accidentally used a phrase or term that had been previously defined as a trigger to a teammate.

By taking the time to learn more about your group *before* you start your work, meeting, or project, and utilizing strategies such as these, you will be creating much needed trust and understanding in your participants.

In Lesson 11, we will further explore how the concept of building trust is imperative to your success. In Lesson 18, we will explore the potential impact of allowing harmful assumptions and biases to continue to exist within our organizations.

LESSON 11

You Need to Encourage Engagement

It Comes Down to Trust

How many times have you led a group meeting and said, "So what does everyone think about ..." only to be answered with complete silence and people looking down at their knees? Why don't people speak up? *Trust* is at the core of the issue. You are asking people to share, without first establishing needed trust in the group. Everyone in the room has their own story, their own past experiences. Have they been bullied for speaking out? Do they typically find themselves silenced by others? Are they willing to share their opinion and risk being shamed and embarrassed by others who may view their idea as *stupid*? In fact, you might be astounded to learn the amount of negative self-talk and self-doubt that are going through the minds of people in your room. In her book *Conflict Management and Coaching,* Cinnie Noble advises that "historical experiences of being provoked or triggered generally tend to taint the impact of the new situation to a greater extent than a single episode. Repeated provocations also typically serve to entrench our judgements and strength on this person or situation" (62). For your members to feel open to sharing, first they need to *trust* that you have their best interests in mind. If not, they may become focused on memories that reinforce their own negative self-talk and not allow themselves to participate. Additionally, if they do speak up, the first time they find themselves shot down, or shrugged off, their self-talk will reinforce their need to disengage.

In fact, *trust* is linked to many core interests of honesty, respect, loyalty, commitment, and integrity. Therefore, trust is not something that many people will give easily. It is one of those fundamental things that is difficult to gain and easy to lose. It also plays a very key role in the definitions of leadership and relationships. It is imperative that trust building occurs first before an organization attempts to deal with sensitive and important issues. I have watched as well-intentioned organizations and groups try to rally people together to discuss issues on diversity strategies, inclusion efforts, practices to introduce new processes and replace old ones, yet have not taken the time to first establish trust. Their efforts tend to result in further mistrust and a failure to move forward rather than their *intended* purpose.

Think back to the last big discussion you participated in. Maybe it was a schedule change, or a new practice or leadership strategy. How well did the discussion go? Could you almost predict who would be willing and open to hear the ideas and who would have their arms crossed and disagree? If you had new people involved in the discussion, were people willing to hear their insight? Cinnie Noble speaks of how negative self-talk can play out neurologically and impact a person's willingness to be involved. "If clients in conflict management coaching concentrate on what went wrong rather than looking ahead with fresh thinking, they stand to remain entrenched in a problem saturated mindset" (*Conflict Mastery* 28). The result may be that the group seems to get nowhere or, in fact, gets even more entrenched in opposing opinions. Little progress is made, and people become stuck in their own stories and opinions.

Building Trust

It is critical that in any activity where we will require people to be vulnerable, share opinions, or examine new ideas, first we need to build trust. It is critical that we spend the needed time to address participants' needs, interests, and concerns with the overall process. By doing so, we help to create more initial trust in the process and the people involved. This results in a better functioning team and greater vulnerability overall.

One strategy you can use to build trust is to have an individual meeting with each of your current team members. Find out what they have enjoyed and/or disliked about previous meetings and then apply the practices learned in Lesson 10 to your meetings. Encourage your team to bring up their "likes and dislikes" at the beginning of the meeting when you ask for suggestions on the "rules of engagement" list you will be creating for the group before you start. You can also incorporate the trigger activity into your group work to provide members further insight into how they can effectively support each other's learning and comfort.

1. Adhere to the Rules

It will be your job as the leader to ensure people adhere to the rules of engagement. Have them typed up or written on foolscap for everyone to see. One skill I learned in mediation is to reference the list if you see behaviours starting to go off course. It is a great way to draw the group's attention back to the list they created together, without shaming anyone. You can say, "I have noticed that you initially wanted to stick to the agenda and discuss the topics in order. You are starting to stray away from that. Is everyone comfortable with reordering the list, or would you prefer we stick to the agenda?" This strategy allows the group to have control of their own process in an organic way, recognizing they may need to change as they go. However, you will also need to ensure everyone's voice is heard. You may use a voting strategy (hands raised) or ask for each opinion before coming to a decision.

2. Addressing Triggers

If you have learned that one of your members is triggered by people who yell and talk over each other, then you will need to ensure that discussions remain respectful and that everyone takes their turn to speak and to hear others. This is often difficult to control when topics become heated and people resort back to their core behaviours. Therefore, a good proactive strategy you can incorporate is the use of a talking stick (also called the speaker's staff). It is an ancient and powerful communication tool that helps to ensure that only the person holding the stick (ball, rock, marker, etc.) may speak. The rest must remain quiet and respectfully listen. It supports the use of a democratic practice to ensure all voices are heard (Indigenous Corporate Training Inc.).

If someone else is triggered by people who immediately shoot down the ideas of others with negative phrasing such as, "we can't, that won't work, that's a stupid idea, we already tried that," then you will need to ensure that everyone understands the purpose of the discussion is to generate ideas, and *no* idea is a bad idea. You will need to encourage participants to hear the ideas of others and build off them rather than dismissing them. You can reinforce this by asking people to paraphrase what they heard the previous person say *before* they start their comments. This helps to engage the brain in listening rather than just reacting to what was heard.

It may seem that this is a lot of extra work and very top heavy for the leader who is just attempting to generate a conversation. But the alternative is that you will hear crickets or only hear from the loud vocal members of the meeting. Either way, your final decision will be the result of limited ideas, and you will not have built trust. In fact, the discussion will continue, but without you present. Discussions around the water cooler, in the lunchrooms, by text, and after work parties will be filled with ideas and criticisms of the final decision! These discussions will then move to bigger conversation on organizational mistrust, fostering an "us and them" mentality, and entrench impressions that processes are unfair, lack transparency, and are about power and control.

Shaming Is Not an Effective Strategy

Building trust does take time, effort, and the need to get to know who you are leading. There is no magic pill or one-size-fits-all solution. Not everyone will have the same needs or fears. You need to learn who they are, what makes them comfortable and what doesn't, and guess what: *They won't tell you unless they can trust that you are not going to exploit this as a weakness and cause them further shame or embarrassment.* It might sound absurd, but I have heard of instances in which supervisors try to crack jokes to get a person to share. Comments like, "Hey, are you going to actually speak up, or just sit there like a mouse? Do you have anything to share?" Yep, that's really going to work. Shaming the person into sharing! Want to guess what happened at the next meeting? They didn't go. Not only did they not want to speak up, but they also didn't even want to risk being called on. They called in sick, they quit the committee, or they made excuses about being too busy to attend.

If you or others use such shaming strategies, slowly your circle of influence to make decisions will become quieter and smaller. Some leaders find that this fits with their own personal authoritative style. They prefer to *tell it how it is* and not be asked to validate their beliefs or ideas. But for those of you in Lesson 4 who preferred a different, more collaborative leadership style, you will need to gain the trust of your employees. This won't happen overnight, but you can start by making the effort to learn more about your team, ensuring no one feels shamed, and challenge yourself to truly meet their needs.

Sharing Builds Trust

Challenge yourself to go back to Lesson 3 and look at your own PI profile or another behavioural assessment you have completed. What could you share with your team about yourself that would help them better understand your intent in asking for input? For example, by explaining that you are social by nature, enjoy collaborative discussions and teamwork, they will start to recognize that you value them as part of the team. This same strategy can be used to also share some of your default behaviours that you recognize may cause issues for others.

For example, by saying to someone "You are very detail-oriented. That is something I am lacking. I need you to speak up to remind me if I have jumped too far ahead in the idea. If my lack of detail is causing you stress, or if I have missed a key element we need to think about, I want you to tell me." This admission helps them to understand that you recognize your own tendency to jump to *action* and potentially miss key details. You are further reinforcing your need to have them help you with this cautionary behaviour and that you see the value of their potential contribution. These admissions and comments will help to build needed trust and contribute to future dialogue.

Encouraging Unique Perspectives

The most creative and progressive processes are built from the ideas of many different, diverse, and unique perspectives. Think back to the historical novel *Hidden Figures* by Margot Lee Shetterly that later became an award-winning dramatic film. The detailed training and knowledge of three African American female mathematicians, known as "computers," helped to change the course of history and launched astronaut John Glenn into orbit. These women battled racism, sexism, and classism as they attempted to get others to listen to their ideas and allow them to share their input. When the white male scientists finally listened, they realized the value and knowledge the Black women had to offer in helping to find the needed solution to launch the space capsule.

Take some time to think about this example.

- What kind of decisions have been made under your leadership that exemplifies this type of blended idea generation?
- Who were involved in the discussions?
- Are there are other discussions that failed to meet the mark?
- What impacted the inclusion or exclusion of needed voices and opinions?

What They Wish You Knew

My survey results provided insight into what employees might wish you knew about them and *why* they haven't told you.

Is there anything you wish you could share about yourself with your supervisor/coach that would help them better understand how to work with you?

Responses:

- Stop multi-tasking and just listen to what I am saying
- Sometimes I need a sounding board, the coach's trusted advice
- Focus on building our team—without a functional team we can't succeed
- When they are distracted, I feel less valued
- Understand that I have a life outside of work
- Microaggressions and biases impact my wellbeing in the workplace
- The impact of workplace stress
- My mental health impacts my job, and I may need help with barriers
- Past traumas, stress, home life all impact me, and being criticized only makes it worse
- I tend to focus more on content that includes visual depictions, so give me detail
- I shared but it didn't enhance our relationship; now the supervisor just leaves me alone and complain to others
- I value constructive criticism coupled with clear steps on how to improve expectations
- I need to feel important for the team to perform better
- When we discuss work hours, I need my boss to stick to the agreed schedule
- I am task- and goal-oriented; if something doesn't impact the task at hand, I don't want to hear about it
- Don't try to "dumb things down for me" to make it easier; challenge me
- I admire innovation and like to think outside the box
- I am judged on my level of education and experience; I feel like I am hitting a brick wall and not given a chance to prove myself
- I want to be able to share without judgement
- I am a little technically challenged and need additional time when working on a laptop
- I am a single mom doing everything solo
- Sometimes the leader needs to step back and let us lead

If you haven't explained this need/interest/personal quality to your supervisor/coach, what is preventing you from doing so?

Responses:

- Work relationship not a friendship
- Won't help or make a difference
- Scared of being criticized or viewed as ineffective
- Pride, courage
- Lack of trust
- Don't think they care
- I don't want to let the team down
- Fear of exposure and being seen as needy and mentally inadequate
- Fear I will lose esteem in their eyes
- They have a very closed-off personality
- It wouldn't be welcomed
- They already know everything
- They respond with "sorry you feel that way" and no useful feedback
- Not an open relationship
- Power imbalance
- Fear of being fired or retaliation

I am very thankful to the people who chose to complete my survey. Their honesty helps all of us reflect and think about those we lead. What information might you be missing? Do you want your employees to be afraid to come forward or feel safe in doing so? How will you support this practice?

Putting It All into Practice

Think about how you can start to put this learning into practice. Instead of just making an agenda of items you wish to discuss at the next meeting, start by writing in the margins. How will you make this meeting a success? What will you do to ensure everyone feels included and heard? Do they need new processes put into place?

Consider these needs and how they can be met:

1. Do team members need time to reflect before the meeting?

- Consider sending the agenda ahead of time.

2. Are some members apprehensive about speaking in a group setting?

   - Consider allowing them to share their ideas via email instead of verbally at the meeting.
   - Allow the group(s) to designate a spokesperson who is more interpersonal and can act as a representative and present their ideas.

3. Do some members feel overpowered by others in a meeting setting and fail to share their valuable insight?

   - Consider the use of a talking stick to allow each member a chance to speak and be heard.
   - Create an idea-sharing process for fifteen minutes before anyone is allowed to move on to action plans and asking questions.

4. What is the size of the group that will be meeting? Are the participants representative of different working groups/teams and therefore may have different concerns or questions?

   - Consider the need to break the agenda up into preliminary sub-meetings to ensure that everyone has a chance to discuss changes/concerns from their perspective and then have a larger meeting to present/discuss the various ideas and approaches.
   - The creation of smaller subgroup discussions also allows people to voice their opinions within their own comfortable team setting.

5. Will you be introducing new processes or systems that may cause initial concerns?

   - Include a well-designed evaluation or follow-up process so that participants know you are willing to hear suggestions and improvements as the process moves forward.

Importance of Check-Ins

Once the meeting is concluded, check back with your individual employees. Reflect on not just the subjects discussed but *how* they were discussed. Ask "How was that meeting for you? Was it any better than the one last week? What else can I change or add to the process?" Some of the responses you get may be hard to hear.

Despite your best efforts, you may receive further criticism: "Well, I thought it was a bit better. I liked getting the agenda ahead of time, but I found Sonja to be very overbearing in the meeting. She always wants to share her ideas first, and I feel overpowered by her. I am afraid she will shut down my idea. I still didn't really feel safe enough to share my ideas. I still have a lot of questions."

Part of you may want to just throw your hands up in the air and say, "Forget it, I give up." But don't. This is actually a massive win. This employee now *trusts* you enough to share what is making them nervous and apprehensive. By telling you they find Sonja overbearing, they are sharing something deeper. You can explore this with them. Start by acknowledging how they felt and apologizing for your misstep in your leadership. "Thank you for sharing. I am sorry I didn't pick up on that and reinforce our rules of engagement. I recognize that Sonja can be overbearing to some and understand how that could be overwhelming to you. I want to ensure you feel safe to engage in our meetings. Would it help if we set some additional guidelines on behaviour, maybe even use a talking stick or virtual hand-raising process to ensure that when one person speaks, everyone listens and doesn't interrupt? Are there any additional items you would like to see added to the conduct rules?" Suddenly you have just empowered that employee to have their own voice and share what would make it easier for them to engage in the meeting. Conduct rules for offices and meetings can be an easy yet powerful way to develop cohesion and reduce power imbalances. It also helps others in the meeting do some self-gauging of their own behaviours and recognize why or how they impact others. You are building a trusting *team relationship*.

In Lesson 12, I will expand on how this concept will further enrich your teams and your leadership. The strategies we build together will enhance your ability to address needs as they arise, instead of trying to fix generational damage and mistrust. This will result in a team that not only grows together but can also model for new employees how to conduct themselves within your organization.

LESSON 12

Healthy Teams Have Healthy Leaders

Creating an Effective Team

A strong and healthy team is the foundation of any organization's success. Leaders need to invest time, training, and energy into the development and maintenance of their teams. Too often we focus on what the team is designed to produce rather than the human dynamics required to make it a success. In his book *The Five Dysfunctions of a Team,* Patrick Lencioni discusses many of the interpersonal and behavioural issues that prevent groups from becoming effective teams. This is a book I have read several times and utilized to develop practices and activities I want to share with you.

Being a Healthy Leader

Creating an effective and healthy team starts with an effective and healthy leader. A hockey team can be filled with skilled players, but without a coach, a mentor, a leader to draw out their individual strengths, facilitate new team play, and work out miscommunications, a team will fail. In fact, we have seen this clearly demonstrated time and time again in many sports, industries, and organizations. An effective and healthy leader committed to their team's success, rather than their own personal agenda or ego, can build a winning team.

Survey responders also highlighted this point with 100% agreement that **effective leadership impacts the success/failure of a team and organization.**

Do you think effective leadership impacts the success/failure of a team and organization?

Impact of Leadership

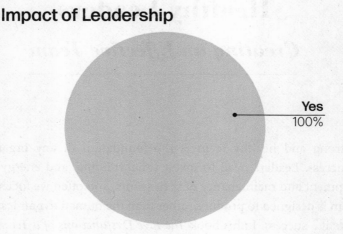

Yes
100%

Creating Team Predictive Analytics

Interestingly, doing assessments with each of your team players can be an extremely effective way to learn more about how they interrelate. Having them then share this information also enhances their ability to understand each other's needs and behaviours. Paired with the MI quiz, the rules of engagement, and the trigger exercise, you will start to develop a very clear image of each teammate and how they impact one another.

At first, you may find people are a little apprehensive to share, and that's okay. Again, it's all about trust. Ensure you have created a safe space to share. Once they start, I find there is often a lot of laughing and *Ah-ha!* moments that come from the learning. What you can discover about your team will help you identify potential outliers and gaps in your team performance. You will start to learn how they work together and how you can more effectively utilize their strengths to enhance the team's success.

An HR counterpart, trained in PI assessments, shared with me an example of how this can play out in a team setting. Their organization had been struggling to try and figure out why an accounting verification team seemed to work so well together but were apprehensive and anxious about working with other teams in the organization. The team became easily frustrated with outside demands, changing priorities, and unclear instructions. Their counterparts, in turn, were frustrated with their seemingly unwillingness to adjust to new demands and needs of the organization. The PI practitioner started by doing everyone's PI. These were mapped onto a Predictive Index team diagram, and the answers became very apparent. The teammates all had very similar behavioural profiles.

Team Assessment

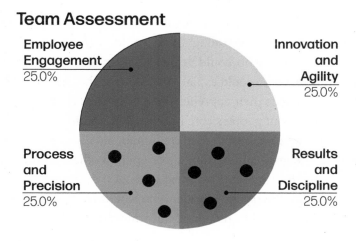

In fact, the teammates literally mirrored one another in their PI assessments and could all be found in the lower two quadrants of the graph. They all liked to work very independently and were very detail-oriented, results-driven, reserved, and extremely risk-averse. They wanted time to audit their work, research the information, and then develop a plan on how to approach the assignment. The work they generated was impeccable, and they functioned very well as a team, but they needed to address the fact that they didn't seem to sync with the organizational needs. This issue is actually quite a common occurrence. As explained in his book *Predicting Success,* Predictive Success cofounder David Lahey highlights that similar job types tend to attract similar personalities, traits, and behaviour preferences (54). We also tend to like to hire people similar to ourselves for our teams. Now think about how this may impact the functionality of a team. Although they were comfortable with each other and how they operated, they did not have anyone on the team who could help them navigate functioning with teams different than themselves. This is an interesting element to consider when developing your own teams. The lack of variation in behavioural profiles on the team caused challenges when they were required to work with people from other groups—their discomfort grew when priorities changed or new projects needed to be accelerated and didn't allow for extended production timelines. They didn't enjoy having to engage with others or change processes mid-stream. The organization had tried to improve the situation by giving them a supervisor who was more of a risk taker, someone who could just "roll with the punches" and easily adapt to change. They thought this would help the group by giving them a spokesperson who could represent their ideas and concerns at meetings, someone who could explain the need for the changing priorities and potentially reduce their apprehension. It didn't work. One of the fundamental things about people's core behaviour and traits is that they don't really change. It represents who they are fundamentally as people. You can learn to bend and grow and become more open to others. However, when you add in stressful situations, we tend to default even more to our core behaviours. So despite having a leader who would try to buffer them and ease them into change, they remained uncomfortable.

Masking Our Core Needs and Behaviours

It is actually very difficult, under pressure, to mask your core needs and behaviours. Here is a quick example to illustrate this point. Let's pretend you need to go to a social event. You really don't want to be there; you don't enjoy most of the people who are going to be in attendance, and the primary entertainment is going to be a live comedian whose act is based on humour you don't really like. How long do you think you will be able to *mask* your behaviours and politely act as if you are enjoying yourself? An hour? It won't be long until you will be sporting a stressful smile and looking for some way to make a polite excuse to leave early and escape. As you walk out the door, you will literally feel an outpouring of relief. It's like kicking off those high heels or loosening that tie at the end of a formal event. You cannot wait to get into your comfy pyjamas and slippers. You want to be in your comfort zone and be yourself. Our work environments are no different. You can give employees a new leader, someone with new and innovative ideas, a cheerleader of sorts who will try and pump them up and encourage that good ol' team spirit, but in the end, people are who they are. In this case, they needed reassurance, steadfast work, and the ability to create their own timelines to produce their well-thought-out and thorough reports.

So Now What?

You may be thinking, *So now what? As organizations we must learn to adjust to our teams that want to take their time and slow down production just to meet their needs? This is ridiculous!*

One of the mistakes we often make is to focus on the team or employee that we, as leaders, see as a problem and try to *fix* them. In the previous example the organization tried:

New supervisor + adjusting to organizational need
= Change the team focus and function.

But it didn't work. The reason can be once again found in Gallup's results on "How to Measure the Strength of a Workplace" found in *First, Break All the Rules.*

Element 9 — Belief that my associates or fellow employees are committed to doing quality work. This brings into question the need to also understand how members may define "quality work." In this case, the verification team had a very high standard when it came to defining quality of work. They knew that if they were required to work too quickly, skip steps, and change priorities, the quality of their work would suffer. So, in fact, their concerns were valid and demonstrated a commitment to mitigating risk for the organization. Additionally, if their concerns were not addressed, the organization risked losing them. Element nine demonstrates that high functioning employees will leave an organization if they feel like others do not share they views.

Having high functioning employees leave an organization is never advantageous. We all know that having to start over creates months of little to no production, stresses out the rest of the team left with more work, and reduces corporate knowledge. Instead, we need to invest in learning ways to create team dynamics that allow for members to feel appreciated, while also addressing the need to inevitably adapt and change.

Helping Teams Understand Each Other

Instead of trying to "change each other," teams need to learn how to work more effectively with each other. Using the team's PI assessments can help you understand *who* they are and *why* certain things are working and some aren't. It will also help to identify why old patterns keep re-emerging and what can be done to change them. This is also where having effective mediation skills comes into play. As a trained interest-based mediator, I enjoy helping employees understand each other's needs in a safe environment and mentoring a conversation in which they can better discuss their needs and interests. Mediation allows individuals and groups to see things from each other's viewpoint and then work together to create some solutions. For example, in the case of our highly formal, detail-oriented verification team who all fell under the behavioural profile of **Specialist**, a mediator would be able to use several different strategies to learn more about the team and their organization and then help them better communicate what they needed moving forward. In the case of this team, their interests were quite straightforward:

- They needed to feel **respected** for the work they did—being rushed and having their priorities changed mid-stream left them feeling disrespected and unable to give the projects the attention they felt they deserved.

- They needed **clarity** and **detailed communication** behind the request—their need for detail caused confusion when instructions were brief and lacked explanation.

- They prided themselves in their work and the **integrity and quality** they put into it—being rushed caused risk of error, and these mistakes resulted in them feeling embarrassed and shamed.

- They needed to be able to **trust** that they wouldn't be blamed if other projects didn't get completed on time due to the changing priorities.

The organization's interests were also quite straightforward:

- They needed to ensure their **reputation** could be maintained— therefore, they often needed reports and data to demonstrate why they had made certain decisions.

- They needed to be able to **trust** that the information they relied on in the reports was accurate and timely—they did not want to be publicly shamed or embarrassed by faulty data.

- They needed the information to be **communicated** to them in a timely fashion—they wanted accurate and defendable information available to them as they tried to address changing circumstances.

Utilizing this information as a starting point, it would allow the groups to then work to create ideas and potential solutions that met the interests and needs of everyone involved.

Ideas:

1. Have a spokesperson who can represent the team at planning sessions to ensure their voices are heard.

2. Using the Lean methodology found in *The Toyota Way*, set priorities and timeline for projects that need to be completed.

3. Requests for new project work can be submitted using a form that will provide the details and information the team requires to understand the scope.

4. Once a project is received, a team lead will be assigned to determine measurable outcomes and timelines so that the organization can know what to expect and when.

5. Create an evaluation process so that all teams involved can provide feedback on what works well and what challenges still exist.

By taking this approach, you enable the team members to feel that you have met three more criteria found in *First, Break All the Rules* and strengthened their belief in the workplace:

Element 7 — My opinion matters.

Element 8 — The mission or purpose of my company makes me feel my job is important.

Element 9 — My associates or fellow employees are committed to doing quality work.

Expanding Team Profiles

By implementing new practices and ensuring that the team feels included and heard, you also increase their willingness to consider adding new behavioural profiles into their fold. Remember, although the team may now see the value in meeting to review new projects and providing evaluation input at the end, it is still not within their comfort zone to want to necessarily be the ones in those meetings and process. They may now see the added value of having others on their team who have strengths in areas of relationship building, collaboration, and decision making. These new members could be assigned the role of attending strategy meetings, bringing back plans to the team, collecting needed information, and consulting with other teams. Together they could effectively work to meet the needs of the verification team and the organization while decreasing the stress on both sides.

In Lesson 13, we will discuss how virtual leadership can also add new challenges to team dynamics and how their needs must also be met.

PART 4

—

PUTTING
LESSONS LEARNED
INTO PRACTICE

LESSON 13

Out of Sight Shouldn't = Out of Mind

Virtual Leadership

At the beginning of 2021, 32% of Canadian employees aged 15–69 worked most of their hours from home, in comparison to only 4% in 2016! (Statistics Canada).

This incredible change to the work environment presents leaders with new challenges when it comes to building trust, communication, and the motivation of employees. We have all had to learn to operate via social media platforms, email, phone, and data-sharing software. In many instances, we will never return to the traditional boardroom setting with leaders physically sitting around a table together. Fully virtual meetings and/or hybrid meetings—in which some members are physically present, while others are joining via computer screen—may well be the norm of the future.

It is therefore imperative that we spend some time examining the concepts developed in this book from this challenging perspective. In fact, I would suggest that leaders need to be even *more* conscious of their behavioural preferences, learning styles, and default behaviours when it comes to leading those they rarely ever meet in person, or in some cases *have never* met!

Virtual Processes Can Become Less Personal

Think about how pre-COVID-19 training sessions or meetings started. Everyone would wander into the room a few minutes early, coffee in hand, and start chatting about their kids, the weekend, holiday plans, and work challenges. After five to ten minutes, the meeting would start and people would inevitably continue to interact and share ideas. You could easily see people's body language, notice if someone was appearing annoyed or starting to disengage. You could make a point of checking in with them after the meeting by getting a coffee together or meeting in a side office.

Now picture that same meeting or training session when pandemic restrictions require work to be virtual, or in contexts where meetings have simply shifted permanently to an online format. Everyone sits alone in their office or at home, in a queue, waiting to be let into the virtual meeting. It generally opens only seconds before it is set to start. There is no casual conversation or sidebar discussions. Hopefully everyone is able to join, their screens don't freeze, their Wi-Fi is strong enough, and they don't lose connection. The leader or facilitator starts speaking and everyone listens. If people have questions, they have to raise their virtual hand and turn on their mic to speak (assuming they have a mic, otherwise they have to add their question to a comment box and hope someone reads it). If people become angry or disengaged, they may just tune out or even turn off their camera. In fact, in some cases cameras remain off for the whole meeting, so participants don't even see each other, let alone actually talk. After the meeting, people immediately log off, because they are scheduled to join another meeting immediately following. No one makes time to chat or have sidebar social conversations.

Thinking back to concepts we have examined so far in this book, how do you think this new way of operating could impact your ability to create effective teams, deal with conflict, identify triggers, or build trust? What risks do you run as a leader? What might you be missing?

Transferring Lessons Learned to a Virtual Setting

Luckily, many of the concepts that have been introduced are easily transferable to a virtual platform. However, it will require leaders to make a concerted effort to include them in virtual practices. Additionally, we need to institute new key proactive strategies to ensure communication and relationships continue to develop and thrive in our new environment.

As you read through the insights from remote workers, listen for their needs and their interests in adapting to and feeling included in this new world. I have provided some specific suggestions on how these needs can be met, but I am sure you will be able to also develop ideas of your own that would best work in your organization.

Setting up for Success

We need to set our employees up for virtual success. For example, our new virtual world requires everyone to have developed a comfort level with technology. In speaking with one remote worker, Dylan, she said this has been one of her biggest challenges.

*I am not technically savvy, so I find a lot of our new processes rather **intimidating**. They sent us all webcams and headsets, with the expectation we knew how to connect them and how to join and interact in the meetings. When I didn't understand where to connect them, they tried to help me verbally over the phone, but as a **visual learner** and not one who is very technical, it just left me feeling more frustrated and embarrassed. I used to be able to reach out to a colleague or IT person to help me in person, but now all of that is gone. I still can't connect properly, so I just don't turn on my camera. It also causes me to **feel less connected** with people.*

As a leader, we need to ensure everyone feels included and able to participate.

Idea: Prior to employees going into remote settings, we need to set them up for success. Set up a meeting for them to speak with your IT people.

Give them an opportunity to discuss Wi-Fi strength, remote desktop set-up, webcam usage, and other issues they may find intimidating.

Idea: Discuss the potential of having IT create a step-by-step video tutorial members can reference if they find themselves unable to utilize the equipment. This type of visual learning is very effective and provides people with a reference point they can use over and over.

Idea: If you notice someone not using a camera, or missing meetings due to faulty connection, check in with them before the next meeting. In helping them solve their issues, or connecting them with people who can help, you are creating trust and feelings of inclusion.

Addressing Learning Styles and Needs

Many of the issues and ideas presented in Lesson 6 on coaching can be utilized to benefit you in a virtual setting when it comes to meeting people's learning styles.

In my conversations with Jordan, he brought up several key factors he finds challenging in virtual teamwork and meetings. Again, as a leader, we need to ensure everyone feels included and able to participate. Listen to Jordan's input and then think about ways you can address it.

*I literally find myself tuning out. I just can't stay focused when someone is just talking on and on about a topic or using a lot of technical terms. It's not that I don't understand its importance, but without the ability to **ask clarifying questions**, or discreetly turn to a colleague who can rephrase a concept for me, I find myself becoming lost. I also really miss out on visually seeing how we are doing something or **how it all fits logically together.***

Idea: Include various ways to present material in meetings. Too often our virtual meetings have become primarily based on verbal dialogue. Our body kinetic, visual, logical, and interpersonal learners are not being engaged.

I find it hard to follow along in meetings. Sometimes I wish we had minutes so that I could refer to them and/or use them as a guide to frame questions

I still have. My boss is just so busy, I don't want to ask general questions or seem incompetent to her.

Idea: Create an agenda and minutes for the meeting.

Idea: Incorporate a question period or process into the meetings so that people know that you are open to inquiries and want them to be engaged.

*One of the things I miss the most is the ability to just sit and chat with colleagues. I loved the **interactive part of working as part of a team**. I used to pick up on things by listening to others or learning about new ways to do things. Now I find I am often out of the loop, and we are all doing things differently and less efficiently, but we don't even realize it.*

Idea: Include time in meetings for "other business" so that employees have a chance to discuss new processes, ideas, or options.

Creating Time for Meet and Greets

Lesson 12 discussed the need to be part of a healthy team. In this example, Kim works in a hybrid work environment. Some of the employees in her work group are in offices located in separate parts of the province, while others work from home. Most meetings involve people who are joining both physically and remotely in a boardroom. She has made it a practice to ensure each meeting starts with a Meet and Greet. A round is done, giving each person a chance to say how they are doing, share a little bit of their personal life if they wish, and others can chime in with "congrats" or "let's chat about that afterwards." As a leader, Kim states it has enabled her to recognize who is emotionally present for the meeting, who seems stressed by work-related or personal matters, and who may need to chat afterwards. Additionally, it provides the team with a few minutes of socializing and normality before the meeting begins.

*My manager allows us to join the meeting a few minutes early. It's nice to have the **ability to check in with each other**, hear about their kids, see where they are living, and hear about some of their struggles. I think in some ways remote work has actually allowed us to blend our work persona and our non-work persona. You can't help it. You are in the middle of a meeting and* *the dog starts to bark. We all laugh. We have learned more about each other, and maybe even some of our **imperfections**.*

Monitoring Interactions

Developing a method to monitor interactions can be a little more challenging in a virtual world. For you, as the leader, trying to pick up on **frustrations, triggers, and disengagement** that may be occurring with your employees will be challenging. Just as we discussed in Lesson 6, it will be imperative that you have done the work to get to know *who* your employees are. It highlights the need to do individual assessments, allowing you to generate a clear understanding of their needs and interests. If you have done this, you will more easily adapt to recognizing some of their default behaviours during difficult and challenging meetings. You will be able to pick up on how some will dominate the conversations, while others will never turn on their mic. Some will speak of high-level conceptual ideas, while others will be frustrated with the lack of detail on how to bring the idea to life. You, as the leader, will need to ensure that processes developed in Lesson 10 and Lesson 12 are utilized to help ensure everyone is feeling included in the discussion.

In other instances, the interactions may be occurring via email and text. No longer are coworkers standing around the water cooler chatting things out. This can inadvertently lead to a lot of **miscommunications** and potentially ones you are unaware of.

Elizabeth shared: *It's so hard to interpret someone's tone in an email. Even after I send an email, I worry about whether the person will read more into it, adding their impressions of my intent when I sent it. You can't read body language or correct someone's interpretation. Often emails are shared, and even more interpretation is added to it. Are they shouting when they add an exclamation mark? Does the fact they didn't even sign off with a thank you mean it's an order and not a request?*

As a leader you will need to find ways to also monitor electronic communication.

Idea: Monitor email chains and watch for signs of miscommunication and/or frustration.

Idea: Offer employees online training in "email etiquette" to help elevate issues.

Idea: Facilitate conversations between members to determine how miscommunications and interpretations have occurred.

Idea: Encourage members to check in with each other by phone or a virtual call if they are unsure on how to proceed or need clarification. This will alleviate the risk of issues growing larger due to ongoing miscommunication.

Doing so will build trust and lessen anxiety as it relates to people worrying that they are being misunderstood and potentially shamed.

Hosting Team Meetings

Initiating weekly or bi-weekly meetings can ensure that as a leader you are able to keep a pulse on what is happening in your team. It will help to address issues of **miscommunication**, **priority setting**, and **work efficiency**. It will allow members to know what others are working on and potentially how they can help out. It is important to ensure that meetings are held with both small team groups as well as larger groups. Remote, virtual settings can easily reinforce the existence of silos and prevent teams from working well together.

Barb introduced a simple but effective method to ensure everyone is able to attend and not feel rushed.

If you have a meeting at the beginning of the day, schedule it 0800–0950. The extra 10 minutes at the end allow for several things to happen:

a. *You have a few minutes to check in and ask questions of someone in the meeting before they rush away.*
b. *You can quickly grab a coffee, tend to other responsibilities, or even have a bathroom break!*
c. *It ensures everyone can stay till the end and still make their next meeting.*

Changing the Rules of the Game

Sometimes we need to re-examine how we are doing things and why. Our virtual world brings with it a whole new set of operational issues. No longer can you just pop into someone's office or run down the hall if you need an update. Colleagues can be globally placed in different time zones. Requests for help must be sent via email and long delays can exist before there is a response. Top-down styles of leadership do not work effectively in this environment.

In Lesson 4, we discussed styles of leadership. **Authoritative leadership** requires leaders to take the time to explain their ideas and set goals and objectives for those they lead, explaining all processes and overseeing the steps it will take to get there. This is a hard task when your employees are in different time zones, working remotely, and must wait for guidance via email. It can cause frustration and despair in the worker who just wants to get things done and takes pride in their work.

Joe, a member of a global mining company, has a clear example of just how frustrating the process can be:

*I work as part of a global team. We have a six-hour time difference. Sometimes I have to wait days for an answer. You can't always wait. I need the boss to have confidence in my abilities and give me the **autonomy** to run things. We are no longer playing the same game, but we want the same results. We must change the rules of the game. Bosses need to allow teams to work together and make decisions. If mistakes are made or people don't follow through, then hold them **accountable**. This must occur at all levels of the organization. If we need a decision from above and they avoid the email or don't give us an answer, then that has to be recognized as an issue and resolved. When the big boss doesn't admit to their own errors, everyone gets disgruntled.*

As leaders, we need to take a hard look at how we are doing things. We need to check in with our employees, learn what is working and what isn't. Most importantly, we need to acknowledge and be accountable for the mistakes we own and rectify them.

Conducting Employee Check-Ins

It has never been more important than now for leaders to take time to check in with their employees. Think about the **need to build trust**. In cases where employees are working remotely, not only do you potentially risk knowing less about them, but the same is true for what they know about you.

This became apparent when I interviewed Shannon on her experience as a remote worker. When I asked if she has ever discussed with her manager what would make her virtual experience better, she answered:

No. I think she is really busy. She only really talks about work issues. I would be nervous to just call her up and talk to her about it. I expect I am the only one really struggling with feeling disconnected and less engaged. I wouldn't even know how to bring it up. I kind of wish we did have individual check-in meetings. Maybe just once every couple of months.

Idea: As a leader, schedule individual check-in meetings with your group members. Explain the intent so that no one is caught off guard and can be prepared to share. These meetings can be hosted virtually, but make sure you can actually see the participants. You need to try and be able to pick up on body language and comfort as part of your assessment in how they are doing. Cover topics such as:

a. Work/life balance
b. Technology
c. Issues and concerns
d. Ideas and suggestions

Idea: Also consider meeting up with employees in an outdoor setting or at a café to allow you to see them, read body language, and pick up on cues you might miss in a virtual setting.

Hosting these individual meetings will create trust and enable you to identify and address many needs and concerns you may have been otherwise unaware of.

Ensuring Work/Life Balance

Despite initial concerns that remote work might reduce productivity, many workers are reporting the exact opposite. A July 2021 report in *The Economist* states, "Remote workers work longer hours, not less."

These concerns were further emphasized by George:

We are literally bombarded with hundreds of emails every day. People think because they sent an email, it's a priority to you. But it's not. You have other issues to deal with, but they can't see that you are already working on something. No one has any patience. It's hard to shut off the computer or ignore the phone at the end of the day. The work just piles up. You never really LEAVE your office. It is right there, and people know it. So the workday gets longer and longer.

It is critical to both your **employees' physical and psychological health** that leaders monitor work/life balance in remote workers. Being at home, trying to juggle family responsibilities, work challenges, longer hours, has taken its toll on people. They are missing out on the social aspects of work that used to make it enjoyable. Work is becoming just work. People are burning out. We need to ensure we are taking this into account.

Idea: Encourage your staff to take a lunch break *away* from the computer, during which they go for a walk, read a book, or play with the kids.

Idea: Encourage meeting participants to stand up and walk around.

Idea: Ensure long meetings include coffee and bathroom breaks.

Idea: Pre-set your emails to go out during *work* hours so that employees don't feel obligated to respond after hours.

Idea: Provide email recipients with realistic timelines for your requests so that they have the ability to prioritize their own work.

Idea: Encourage employees to contact you if they are feeling overwhelmed by conflicting demands from different departments so that you can assist them with determining priorities.

Introducing Social Meetings and Events

In a virtual world, we run the risk of people not feeling part of anything. For those employees whose behavioural needs include **socializing and being stimulated through conversation and relationship building**, remote work can be extremely isolating. Colleagues become just a name on an email rather than someone you consider a friend and confidant. Therefore, it is extremely important that organizations and leaders find ways to ensure their employees feel part of the organization. In fact, this is key to retention. If you feel part of an organization, feel a commitment to the team, and feel like you belong, you are more likely to stay.

Zoey shared how her employer had created **social meetings** designed to help employees get to know each other better.

Once a month, we have a one-hour scheduled social meeting. It's during work hours (not lunch), and people meet to share about their personal interests, accomplishments, family struggles, and even share pictures and show craft items. Anything goes. The only rule is "no shop talk"—you can't discuss work issues. If someone starts to, they are asked to schedule a separate meeting for that topic. At first, I was a little hesitant, but it's actually fun. It has allowed me to feel reconnected with some of my colleagues. We have ended up sharing meal plans, recipes we like, and how to deal with parenting issues.

Devon expanded on this idea with the creation of social virtual events.

We created a virtual Halloween event … Everyone showed up in costume. We also have game events where we play Pictionary or bingo. It's easy to do virtually and creates lots of laughs. We need it. Otherwise, you just feel like a robot. You don't even have to drive into work anymore. You just come down, turn on the computer, login, and start working. You don't interact with anyone except by email. It can be long and very disengaging. This brought back some of the fun we were missing.

Jack added:

We held an ugly-sweater contest for our virtual Christmas event. We had over 200 people in attendance. The big boss spoke, managers highlighted work their teams had accomplished, and we had some fun doing it.

LESSON 13

Sending Special Deliveries

Organizations have gotten very creative in finding ways to ensure their employees **felt appreciated and connected**. For example, during the Christmas holidays, Chris's employer had deliveries sent to their employees' homes. The packages included a gift basket the whole family could enjoy, and all of the ingredients needed to create a gingerbread house! Families then met virtually to share their house creations. Given that it was an architectural firm, you can only imagine the creativity and talent that went to some of those homes!

There are many other ways that leaders can invest in their virtual and hybrid teams. Doing so will not only help to ensure that you are getting to know *who* you are leading, but also ensure you are meeting their needs in a virtual setting. This effort can potentially build stronger teams that meet the needs of both your employees and organization.

LESSON 14

Don't Offer Solutions

Conflict Is Inevitable

How much time do you think you invest in trying to resolve workplace conflict? A recent study showed that between 30–42% of a manager's time is spent mediating disputes between coworkers (Rapid Learning Institute). It is exhausting, frustrating, and often unsuccessful. After spending years in HR—and even more years supervising, coaching, and working with people in conflict—I have realized that we need to dig much deeper in order to ensure we are addressing the underlying issues. I have also discovered that without the necessary training, managers are ill-equipped to try and resolve long-standing conflict. For years, I had no idea how to effectively address conflict. I would try to simply hear the issues, offer solutions, and hope for the best. It wasn't until I took my interest-based mediation training that I realized how much I was missing.

Your Conflict-Resolution Skills Don't Go Unnoticed

If we don't resolve conflict effectively, it *doesn't* go unnoticed by our employees. Survey results confirmed this same finding.

Does your supervisor/coach help to address conflict or issues of concern you have with other members? Only 58% of the employees indicated yes.

139

Addressing Conflict

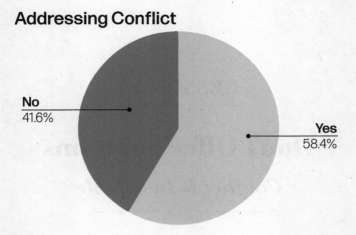

No
41.6%

Yes
58.4%

Additionally, employees also take time to notice what methods are being used to resolve issues.

Are the techniques the coach/supervisor use to address conflicts/ concerns effective? Employees responded:

YES

- Encourage and empower communication among members
- Set up meetings to address conflict
- Validate steps I plan to use and offers suggestions/wording
- Frank, honest, one-on-one conversations
- Identify unmet needs, offer suggestions
- Facilitate dialogue and use organizational HR processes
- Gentle communication
- Group discussion to identify "larger issues" without using any-one's names
- Use mediation skills to learn what drives ambition, personality, and root issues
- Intervene to ensure we have a safe, learning work environment
- Bosses get both sides of the story and then institute discipline if necessary

KNOWING WHO YOU LEAD

NO

- Avoid conflict at all costs
- Struggle with conflict not knowing how to address it
- Usually tell us to work it out
- Bosses side with "pet" employees over anyone else
- Small team, so no one wants to bring things up
- Tell us to "shut it down and work it out"—they are not our babysitters

Clearly there is a need for leaders not only to address conflict but also to develop effective ways to do so.

The following is an example of a typical workplace conflict that almost every leader has experienced. Jan walks into your office and before she can barely shut the door she has burst into tears. She says she has had it with Darryl and can't handle working with him anymore. She wants you to change his working group assignment so that she no longer has to work with him. She is tired of him interrupting her work with questions, pointing out her errors, telling her what to do, and gossiping about how inept other colleagues are. What are your initial inner thoughts? *(It's okay, I won't tell anyone ... just be honest.)*

a. Here we go again. I can't move Darryl. No one can work with him.

b. I am not a babysitter. Just do your work and ignore him!

c. Maybe I can move Jan and that will help.

d. If I talk to Darryl, he will book off "mad" and we can't afford to lose him.

Sound familiar? In fact, most workplace conflicts fall under the same type of criteria:

1. Jealousy of others
2. Performance issues
3. Power struggles
4. Miscommunication (rumours)
5. Pride/ego

Getting to the Root of the Issues

Interpersonal conflict amongst employees often has very deeply rooted issues linked to past behaviour and interactions, and they are not easily resolved. However, our typical managerial way of dealing with them tends to be solution-based rather than interest-based. Hence the "solutions" are often short term, cause more resentment, and the issues keep coming up time and time again. That's why you will hear people say, "he's always been an issue." No one has really figured out what is behind the emerging issues or been able to effectively use the correct tools to help both Darryl and Jan learn more about themselves and each other. Let me explain.

Think back to what you have learned so far about the PI assessment. If we were to assess Darryl, what might we find? Not sure? Right! Because you don't know enough about him yet, so let me share some insight.

Darryl has been employed with your organization for 20 years. He is highly skilled at what he does. He fits the profile of a **Scholar**. He is detail-oriented and very dependent on policy and procedure. His colleagues describe him as "black and white," and he has a strong dislike for change. He is easily stressed if the rules are bent for other employees or if people suggest other ways of doing things. He has high expectations for his own quality of work and those around him. With all of his knowledge and skill, he would be an excellent coach, except for the fact that he is fairly reserved and has little patience for what he terms "lazy and sloppy employees." You have already had many chats with him about how he interacts with others in the office, and you have moved him from group to group trying to keep everyone happy. Nothing works. If he discovers errors in others' work, he will point it out to them. He will cite procedure and "school them" on what they should have done. In some ways he is your ideal employee. When you are not there, he runs a tight ship. He calls people out on laziness and reports if people are taking long breaks or not "pulling their weight." The issue is no one wants to work with him, and now Jan has come to you.

Jan is a new employee. She has been with you for about two years. She has a beautiful smile and bubbly personality. She bakes cakes for people's birthdays (even Darryl's) and is very well liked by her colleagues. She is a

Persuader. She does her work well and often brings forward suggestions and ideas on how to improve archaic processes. She is innovative and loves to think outside the box. She gets along with everyone, is a team builder, and does not engage in office gossip. You see her as an up-and-comer who will likely someday be a coach or even supervisor. Now she is talking of leaving the organization. She has heard from others that Darryl has been like this for years and nothing is being done about it. She is skeptical that you can make any real change. She feels unsupported and believes you favour Darryl over the other employees.

So now what? Basically, we have two completely different employees who can't stand working with each other. What would be your typical solution?

a. Move one to a different group.

b. Give Darryl an independent auditing assignment that he will excel on and not have to interact with people.

c. Advised them to talk it out and try to resolve their own differences.

d. Tell them just to ignore each other.

How long before the next employee or Darryl is at your door complaining about the same issues? A week? (*Maybe, if you are lucky.*) What do you do this time? The behaviour doesn't really breach any of your respectful workplace policies or workplace harassment policies. Do you focus on performance? In this case, Darryl is acting by pointing out errors in others' work. So do you discipline the others for their failed performance? Do you focus on Darryl's gossiping and the fact that it is causing a toxic workplace? What is he gossiping about? People's poor performance? Should you discourage this or reward it? If you don't improve the workplace environment, employees will leave and the whole vicious cycle will start over again.

Feeling Overwhelmed as a Supervisor

It's not hard to feel overwhelmed as a supervisor or leader when it comes to workplace conflict and the issues it brings forward. I think, if we are honest, we have all found ourselves ready, at times, to just hand in our managerial title and say, "I didn't sign up for this. I just wanted to do a higher level of work; I didn't want to become a counsellor. None of my leadership training is working. I have been an empathetic listener, I have tried to find solutions, and nothing changes. I am not their parent! I just need them to get along and do their work and help me get the job done."

In fact, most of these issues are recognized in the "Top 12 Common Management Challenges" that impact your ability to lead your team:

1. Decreased performance levels
2. Being understaffed
3. Lack of communication
4. Poor teamwork
5. Pressure to perform
6. Absence of structure
7. Time management
8. Inadequate support
9. Skepticism
10. Difficult employees
11. Transition from co-worker to manager
12. Weak workplace culture

The article, written by the Indeed Editor Team, goes on to highlight ways you can attempt to address each of the 12 issues. Under "difficult employees," it suggests listening to the issues, finding solutions, and enlisting the support of your HR department. And this is exactly what most managers do. Many times, I have had supervisors and managers call to say, "Can we chat about an issue I am having?" I have had many such discussions. We meet to discuss what they have tried so far, what they can do, and how to ensure their efforts are documented to protect both themselves and the organization should the issues become bigger. In many cases, small disputes over work assignments, personality clashes, respectful behaviour, and gossiping can be resolved by the manager. But in other cases, we would soon discover the issues are less about the "issue at hand" and more about *who* the people are you are dealing with. Often when I would ask, managers didn't really know enough about their employees to figure out what the underlying issues were. Or if they did know them, they weren't sure what they could share with the other employee to help create empathy and understanding.

Using Interest-Based Mediation Skills

This is where I learned to blend my mediation skills with my PI training to help create that pathway of understanding. It helped both employees and supervisors learn more about *why* the issues might be occurring in the first place. I would meet with the supervisor and both parties involved. By overlaying their PIs and objectively explaining their different interests and behaviours, suddenly the picture became a little clearer. Having the two of them in the office together and visually showing them the differences can ease a lot of tension and reduce blame.

Jan (Persuader)—Strengths	Darryl (Scholar)—Strengths
Enjoys risk and thinking outside of the box	Data-driven, analytical, and disciplined
Extraverted, leading, and motivating	Introspective, works independently
Delegates work and enjoys variety	Deliberate with desire to master subjects
Enjoys freedom from structure	Organized, stable, and consistent

Let's go back to Jan and Darryl and see what happens if we try this strategy:

Jan now understands that her love for change and offering new suggestions for how things can be done causes Darryl a lot of internal stress. His need for steadfast processes and policies conflicts with her love for thinking outside the box. Jan now realizes that Darryl's ability to put policy into practice with incredible detail and precision is an asset, not an annoyance. In fact, she is already thinking about ways this could benefit her. If she wants to compete for the next supervisor role, she will need to learn the policies the way he has. She realizes that she could change the way she feels about his auditing her work and his questions. Instead of seeing them as threatening and judgmental, she could consider that his insight might actually be beneficial. Darryl, in turn, realizes that his "matter of fact way of saying things and asking questions" probably comes across as harsh. He shares that he has always had a hard time making friends in social environments, and he is in fact a little jealous of how much everyone likes Jan. The safe sharing allows him to open up and mention that he loves the fact that she is so considerate and included him in the birthday cake celebrations. Darryl goes on to say that he is not opposed to new ideas. In fact, one of Jan's ideas to create a shared-task list for the group was very productive and created huge efficiencies. He also pointed out that this list now allows him to monitor who is doing what, and who is *not* pulling their weight! *As a supervisor you will need to address this issue and ensure you are taking the lead on addressing underperforming staff so that Darryl doesn't feel the need to. By doing so, you will be meeting his needs and also identifying others' needs.*

As an organizational mediator and coach, I would then move into a discussion on interests. What do they each need so that we can try to work on potential solutions?

Darryl starts:

"I need Jan to share her ideas on new processes in some detail and then give me time to think about them and research whether they will work in our current processes. Her excited way of talking about big ideas with little detail makes me really anxious. I just need to make sure we are not compromising detail or are potentially at risk of causing more errors by implementing new processes."

Jan smiles and nods. "That seems fair."

As a mediator, I would reframe this "need" as **detailed communication** and **time to review**.

Jan adds her needs:

"I need Darryl to work on how he tells me about my mistakes. He's so smart, it is intimidating. I feel like he is looking down on me. I would prefer he puts his thoughts into a friendly email and then is open to me asking for clarification or coaching. I don't want to be told what to do; I want to learn."

Darryl smiles for the first time. He laughs and says, "Yeah, I can work on that."

Again, I help to reframe the need for **respectful communication** and **opportunities to learn**.

When we take these new interests/needs into consideration, we realize that our original solutions would not have met any of the needs. We would have completely missed the mark if we had:

e. Moved one to a different group

f. Given Darryl an independent auditing assignment that he would excel at and not have to interact with people

g. Advised them to talk it out and try to resolve own their differences

h. Told them just to ignore each other

Instead, now seeing the interests for what they are, and understanding more about *who* Darryl and Jan are, we can focus on finding new solutions. In fact, Darryl and Jan will be the ones, through facilitated conversation, who will often come up with their own solutions.

Facilitating New Solutions

1. Darryl is going to go back and re-read some of his recent emails to Jan criticizing her work. He has asked if he can take an online course on email composition and etiquette to learn how to integrate coaching and more empathetic language into his correspondence.

2. Jan wants to set up a time at the beginning of their shifts to review the emails and have Darryl coach her on how to prevent the errors.

3. Jan has agreed to no longer come to Darryl with her underdeveloped ideas for new processes. She will work with the manager to better develop the idea into an actionable process and then give it to Darryl in a written format so that he can review it. A meeting will then be set to review the idea and determine next steps.

4. Darryl has offered to put together a training manual on "common errors" that can be prevented. This manual will be provided to new trainees to help in their training.

5. As the manager, you also have agreed to start monitoring the team task list and speak to those who are underperforming.

6. Darryl has agreed to come to you with concerns he may have about other employees and not engage in office gossip.

The additional bonus is other coworkers will inevitably notice the lessening tension between Jan and Darryl. Given Jan's ability to collaborate and comfort with social interaction, she may also become a buffer for Darryl and help others understand him better. This in turn helps him start to feel he is part of the team and make a greater effort to engage with people in the manner of: "I'd like to teach you rather than *tell* you what to do." As a manager, you will hopefully have more time to focus on your own work while promoting the strengths that both Darryl and Jan bring to your unit.

Don't Let Ego Get in the Way

Interpersonal conflict is not only inevitable but also needed. In her book *Conflict Mastery: Questions to Guide You,* Cinnie Noble tells us that "interpersonal conflict provides an opportunity to learn and grow. It allows us to better understand and empathize with ourselves and those with whom we live and work. Positive conflict is a mindset that accepts differences without having or needing to find fault or attribute blame. It is about seeing whether we are able to bridge the gap that exists between our disparate views and ways of interacting with one another" (9).

I think effectively addressing conflict is a key learning moment for leaders. Think about conflicts *you* have had in the past with coworkers. Have you taken the time and effort to get to the root of the issues, the disagreement, or the conflict? Did you regress into a dark space where your ego took over and you needed to find fault or blame? I think if we were to take a true, unhampered look at most of our conflicts, we all own a piece in them. We have all made mistakes. Ryan Holiday's book *Ego Is the Enemy* brings this concept to life very effectively. "The problem is when we get our identity tied up in our work, we worry that any kind of failure will then say something bad about us as a person. It's a fear of taking responsibility, of admitting that we might have messed up. Ego asks, *Why is this happening to me? How do I save this and prove to everyone I'm as great as they think?* It's the animal fear of even the slightest sign of weakness. You've all seen this. You've all done this. Fighting desperately for something we're only making worse" (189).

The only way you will build *trust* with your team and build a willingness in others to address their conflicts is if *you* do it first. Take a few minutes and think back to recent (or even not so recent) conflicts/disagreements you have had with others.

- What does that unresolved conflict prevent you from doing?
- Is it hampering your growth or the growth of others?
- Does it impact others around you?
- Does it prevent teams from effectively working together?
- Does it cause others to feel the need to "pick sides" or pick allegiances?
- Does it demonstrate the type of leader you want to be?

It's Never Too Late

It's never too late to resolve conflict. Conflict can always be looked at and re-examined. Use some of the tools you have learned so far in this book. Think about your interests and needs that were at the root of the conflict. Think about how your behavioural traits may have contributed to a failure in communication or even a power struggle. Now think about how you can re-open the dialogue. How does your counterpart best learn and deal with conflict? If you don't know, ask a trusted colleague. You may want to involve a neutral third party to facilitate the conversation or write out your thoughts in an email first. The key is to open the door to dialogue with the understanding that it is *not* to blame, shame, or find fault, but rather to learn, grow, and rebuild a needed relationship. If you make this effort as a leader, others *will* notice. Lead by example and work to regain the important insight that those *different* from yourself can contribute to your life.

LESSON 15

Listening Is a Developmental Skill

What Did YOU Say?

L et's be honest ... most of the time, we really aren't listening to what other people say. Sometimes we are just too busy to care, and other times it's the *source* of the information. Are there people in your life who are easier to listen to and others who just make you cringe? Are there times when you find it easier to listen, and times when it is an utter annoyance?

Ximena Vengoechea's book titled *Listen Like You Mean It: Reclaiming the Lost Art of True Connection* introduces some important concepts when it comes to listening that can be powerful and applicable lessons for leaders as we try to get to know *who* our employees are.

Default Listening Modes

Vengoechea outlines the concept that we all have default listening modes. They can be influenced by our unique temperament, how we have been socialized, and even cultural expectations. She lists twelve common default listening modes that emerge when we are talking and listening to others.[8]

---

8   To learn more about these listening modes, I highly recommend you read *Listen Like You Mean It* in its entirety.

The **Explainer** has an answer to everything.

The **Validator** is a natural cheerleader and may inflate your ego and skew your perspective.

The **Identifier** likens their experience to yours and brings the conversation back to them.

The **Problem Solver** has a solution for everything and is the perfect sounding board when you need to make progress or improve an idea.

The **Nurse** puts your needs above theirs. All the caring can get overwhelming.

The **Defuser** plays down tense or uncomfortable situations, often using jokes.

The **Mediator** looks at things from all angles, but sometimes makes you feel unsafe to share your point of view.

The **Empath** reads cues on how you are feeling or reacting and may unintentionally make you feel exposed.

The **Interrupter** is always one step ahead. They can make spirited but tiring conversationalists and may make you feel shut out.

The **Interviewer** is genuinely curious; they ask a lot of questions and may make the conversation feel like an interrogation.

The **Daydreamer** is often lost in thought during conversations and is easily distracted.

After reading the descriptions, which one resonates with you? Think of interactions you have at work and at home. Are you getting the most out of conversations, are you learning what you need to learn, or are you hijacking yourself?

When I read this, it immediately struck me how these listening styles also linked to our PI profiles. As an independent, self-starting, social, risk-taking **Maverick**, I am definitely a **Problem Solver**. When I think about how I listen to people's issues, it strikes me that I often want to try and help them solve problems. As Vengoechea outlines, this can be both a blessing and a curse. Problem-solving listeners may have the tendency to try to jump in, ask closed-ended questions, and get to the issue at hand in order to help the person.

Developing Enhanced Listening Skills

We can all benefit from developing enhanced listening skills. After reading my confession about being a default problem solver, you might be thinking: Is this a smart thing for a mediator to be admitting to? Isn't the purpose of mediation to just neutrally facilitate the conversation and do more *listening* than talking? How good can you be if you are already focused on trying to solve the problem at hand? Didn't you already teach us that we shouldn't just jump to conclusions, and that what we often think is the needed solution is the wrong one?

You are right, but don't slam the book down yet. Let me explain. This is in fact the beauty of leaders having the courage to be vulnerable, admit to their faults, and become curious about what else they can learn. Vengoechea makes another interesting point in her book. She equates learning to listen better to learning to be a more effective speaker. If we can learn to speak more effectively, why can't the same apply to listening? How many people do you know who were, at one point, terrified to speak in public settings? I have met many. One of the courses I teach is on giving effective presentations. So often I would have people come to the class on the first day only to confess they were "voluntold" to come and hated presenting. They dreaded the idea of stepping up in front of a class, potentially drawing a blank, stumbling over their words, turning beet red, and sweating profusely. Worse yet, now they were being asked to subject themselves to this in front of a group of peers. They were convinced they would fail miserably. Luckily for me, they didn't fail (otherwise my course would have been very short lived). These people all had been selected for the course because they had a unique expertise in their field. We wanted them to feel comfortable enough to present at training sessions and at conferences. I just needed to convince them to believe in themselves and give them some easy tools to apply to help alleviate the nerves.

We started out slowly. I invited them to talk about a topic they knew well, for one minute, while remaining seated. This immediately helped to eliminate some of their initial fears—they weren't at the front of the room, the presentation was only sixty seconds, and the topic was their choice. Everyone was supportive and helped to ease the tension. As we progressed through the course, we practiced presenting in groups with each person taking on the portion of the topic or demonstration they were most comfortable with. They learned how to practice their subject ahead of time, recording themselves so they could later see "it wasn't that bad." Integrating group activities, questions, and videos helped to lengthen the presentation without requiring them to talk the entire time. After the course was complete, I would make myself available to participants who wanted to work on their "real presentations" or debrief after a particularly stressful one. Years later, I have watched these same people excel at speaking engagements, handle tough questions, and confidently present their material.

Finding Ways to Practice

So why can't we apply this same concept of practice to developing listening skills? The key is not to throw ourselves into really tough situations right away; we have to learn and practice the new skills in safe situations first. We need to practice our skills with people whom we trust and who are willing to point out when we are falling back into old habits (picking up our phone, looking at the computer, asking closed-ended questions, interrupting them). By doing so, we will learn how to become more effective in our listening. I have taught myself to increase my listening abilities as a mediator and an **Empath**. I want to ensure that I relate to how the situation is impacting people, see all sides, generate discussion, and encourage *them* to engage in their own problem solving.

Try this: The next time you go to a party or social event, try just listening. Challenge yourself not to dominate the conversation, not to offer your opinions, not to interrupt. If you tend to be someone who doesn't engage in conversation, a **Daydreamer**, or someone that shies away from social interaction, then challenge yourself to actually listen to the conversations and not just try to hide in the corner wishing the event were over. In either case, it is actually harder than it sounds. If you are an **Interviewer** or an **Interrupter**, then *bite* your tongue and don't engage until it is needed. Just listen.

Staying Grounded

Just like in all the other lessons, we are realizing that many of the skills, training, and knowledge we have developed as leaders need to be integrated and combined to be truly effective. The same is true with developing listening skills. If we are going to be able to institute listening skills and use them to learn more about those who work with and for us, then we also have to integrate some of our previous learning about triggers, needs, and default behaviours into our practice so that we can set ourselves up for success. This was one of the first lessons they taught us in mediation. As the mediator, we need to be feeling grounded and open to doing the work. We learned that if we are having a rough day, are triggered by other things happening in our life, we shouldn't mediate on that day. This rule is also true for those participating in the mediation. Everyone needs to be open to the experience and willing to listen if it is going to work.

Example:

Just prior to one of our mediation practice sessions, I had been dealing with some really stressful situations at work. Without realizing it, I was extremely defensive. I was supposed to play a participant role in a mock mediation, be slightly argumentative, and then move to being open to working with the other person to help resolve the issue at hand. Instead, I was very reactionary to every idea the other "player" was introducing into the scenario. I was *not* actively listening to what they had to say and instead became defensive and short tempered. While it did challenge the mediator to try and figure out how to bring this combative, defensive participant back online, it really wasn't the purpose of the exercise. I was supposed to be allowing her to practice her transition skills, moving from being positional and solution-based to actually hearing one another and developing mutual understanding about our needs. I did both her and the other participant a disservice by not recognizing I wasn't in the right headspace to mediate that day. This was a very important lesson for me. I realized that I am much more open to instituting my learning and listening skills if I am feeling grounded.

In this case, I needed to have my own personal needs and interests met first **(feel validated, have autonomy)** before I tried to interact with others. This is a very real scenario and one that leaders need to be conscious of. We are only human. We have our own issues, needs, and interests. Make sure that you are finding the support you need so that you are, in turn, able to show up for others the way they need you to. If you are having a rough day, be vulnerable and willing to explain that you need to reschedule so that you can be openly present to hear and work through the issues at hand. We are all human. Remember Anna's words in lesson 7? "Be kind to yourself." Sometimes we just need to put our needs first so that we have time to rebound and be there for others.

Delivering Bad News

Think about times you have been required to deliver bad news. Maybe an instance when you had to tell someone they didn't get the job, they didn't do well in a performance review, or you need to enforce a disciplinary action. What is your default behaviour? Typically, we might equate this to how you are going to orally deliver a message (lots of detail or lots of emotion), but it can also apply to what you will typically *listen* for in the conversation and how you may potentially react to what you hear.

Scenario 1:

You need to tell someone about a decision that you have made that will impact them. Maybe you are going to tell them they are fired, or that you won't be selecting them for the position. Maybe it's a friend and you need to explain why you can't go on the trip or invest in their project. In preparing for the conversation, what do you focus more on?

a. Ensuring I have the details and facts correct so that I can properly describe/defend my decision

b. Focusing on *how* I will deliver the message, because I am concerned with how they will react

c. Both are equally important

While "c" is true, most people will find they are more objective or more relationship based. If the person is objective based, they may rehearse how they will tell the person, and what evidence or facts they will use to ensure the response can be substantiated. If they are more of an empathetic person, they will focus more on the tone of their voice, the setting, and how they will react if the person becomes upset. As leaders who need to deliver the bad news, we need to become very conscious of both the delivery and the words we use. We need to become conscious of what we are "listening for" in their reaction and how we will address it.

Here is an example that will help to expand on this concept:

Jill is a **Collaborator**. She loves to interact with others and build relationships. People often tell her she puts others first too often and is at risk of burning herself out. She will always go the extra mile and tries to avoid conflict. She focuses on the subjective part of a conversation and wants to ensure the person feels validated. As a member of the interview panel, she has been tasked with telling Terri, a five-year employee, that he did not get the promotion he was hoping for. She is really worried about how she will deliver this bad news. She knows that the employee has a young family and just purchased his first home. The increased income that went with the new promotion would really help. As Jill prepares to deliver the news, she thinks about the words she will use. She wants the message to be soft and friendly, and she is afraid she may get emotional if Terri is angered by the news.

Jill: *Hi, it's great to see you today. How's everything?*

Terri: *Good. I am super nervous about this meeting. I am really hoping it's good news. I need the money for our new house. There were a few extras issues we didn't know about, so we are really maxed out.*

Jill: (Immediately rattled, she hears the hope in his voice and doesn't want to disappoint him. She focuses on how this message she is about to deliver may make Terri feel. She starts her explanation.) *Oh wow. I am so sorry to* *hear that. Buying a house can be so stressful. So, yes, I did want to talk to you about the position. It was a really tough competition with some great candidates. You really impressed the interviewers with your knowledge and skill. The panel thought you did really well. The only issue was the fact that there were a lot of great candidates. The panel even tried to determine if we could offer more than one promotion, but for now it doesn't seem like we can, but we might be able to in the future. You are such a great employee, and you have a lot to offer us.*

Terri: (Looking confused.) *So I got the position?*

Jill: *Well, unfortunately we didn't have the ability to promote more than one. But you did really well in the interview. I am so sorry.*

Terri: (Now he hears sadness and disappointment in her voice) *So I did really well, but didn't get the job. I don't get it?*

Jill: *Well, you all did well. You are great candidates. It was a hard decision. I am so sorry. Maybe we can talk about other options or ideas.*

Terri: (Reacting in anger and frustration.) *This is BS. I have been here for five years. You said I work hard and have the skills. I don't understand why I didn't get it. I thought I rocked that interview. I will be filing a grievance.* (Terri gets up and leaves the office angrily.)

Jill is shocked by the sound of his anger. She had tried to be so empathetic. She had used the "sandwich approach" she learned in leadership training to deliver the bad news. She had praised him for his skills, told him he didn't get the position, and then tried to give him hope for the future. Why hadn't it worked?

Jill now comes to you, as her supervisor, to try and remedy the situation before a grievance is filed. She is upset and looking for guidance and reassurance. You realize you will need to work to rebuild her self-confidence as well as help her grow in this skill.

Let's unpack this example:

There is a lot to take into consideration. If you are a detail-driven leader, you will likely approach the questions from more of a fact-finding mission focused on right and wrong versus a collaborative-based leader who will be more concerned with the relationship-building impact this situation could have on the organization. Neither is wrong. In fact, a balance would be ideal. Therefore, this is something you need to keep in mind as you progress through the investigative process.

This is a perfect example of how as leaders we need to combine many of the different skill sets we have learned and then use them to address issues. Before you try and figure out how to address it, you need to consider *who* is involved. What do you know about Jill, Terri, and the other interviewers in question? Was everyone being objective in their marking?

By first examining all of these facts and details, you will be in a better position to sit down with Terri to discuss the matter. Before you do so, quickly refer to Lessons 10 and 11. By taking into consideration trust issues, triggers, needs, and behaviours, you will be able to have a more productive conversation with Terri. Here's what you may want to look at:

1. Terri's interview marks in comparison to those of other candidates. How did he rate? Review his answers in comparison to the others. What is the difference?

2. Jill's preference to collaborate and address the emotional impact of the message may have made it slightly more vague and less detailed than Terri needed.

3. Terri's needs for **financial security**, as well as feeling **respected** by the panellists.

4. The reality that Terri is now disgruntled and may file a grievance that will cause a delay in the needed promotion and potentially impact his productivity and loyalty to the company.

5. Who was selected for the position, and did they objectively earn it? If so, then a grievance will likely be unsuccessful, but Terri will still be angry.

Things to Consider:

Once you have assessed this information, how will you use it to repair the miscommunication and Terri's reaction to it? Additionally, you may also want to consider asking if Jill can be present for the meeting. This will offer you the opportunity to mentor her and allow her to grow in her skills.

When you meet with Terri, listen to what his concerns are and don't immediately go into problem solving or justification, even if you know the answers. He will need to feel heard and need you to validate his concerns.

- If he feels that the process was flawed, or the marking was unjust, then the research you did prior to the meeting will allow you to offer needed, objective information.

- If he feels he didn't get to say everything he wanted to in the interview, this can also be a great interview-coaching opportunity. Often debriefing the actual interview with candidates allows one to better understand what they can do to improve their own chances at success.

Your intent in meeting with Terri was to allow him to hear the message correctly, with the detail that he needed, so that you can both move forward. He will still be understandably disappointed with the outcome; however, you can now work together to encourage him to try again.

In Lesson 16, I will expand on this concept and demonstrate how to boost morale in those who have failed and learn a lot more about the people you work with.

LESSON 16

Focus on WHO They Are, Not Just WHAT They Can Do
I Thought I Had a GREAT Interview

How many times have you left an interview thinking "I rocked that" only to find out you didn't?

Have you ever had to debrief people after an interview only to be baffled by how well they thought they did, when in reality their responses fell flat and lacked detail?

Have you had to interview the same person for multiple jobs, yet each time they failed to improve their delivery and answers? It can be a frustrating process for both you and them.

As you know, part of being an effective leader is helping to ensure that you develop and mentor those around you to grow and expand in their own skills. In fact, your retention of employees depends on it. Jim Harter, PhD, describes this further in his book *First, Break All the Rules* based on Gallup research on the most effective managers. Statistics show that employees will only stay with an organization 2.4 years before they consider leaving. Gallup research expanded this concept to consider why people stay. After 25 years of research, and interviewing more than a million employees, certain patterns started to emerge that truly measured the core of a strong workplace.

Results indicated that people want their managers to:

- Select a person
- Set expectations
- Motivate the person
- Develop the person

Insight from Interview Coaching

As I spent more time in HR, I realized that so many excellent candidates just weren't excelling at interviewing. Not enough people knew how to expand on their answers, ensure they actually answered the question, or emphasize why they would excel at the job they were applying to. I decided to start coaching in order to help people succeed in their interviews. My business—which includes one-on-one coaching, online courses, an e-book, and free YouTube videos—is designed to help people increase their understanding of how to prepare and how to bring across their most authentic and unique self in an interview. To learn more, visit my website at www.jobinterviewcoach.ca. The experience has been as enriching for me as it has been for my clients. I have learned so much about what motivates people, how they interact with others, and what holds them back from being successful. In *First, Break All the Rules,* Harter suggests that "many people don't know what their true talents are. When asked, *what are you good at? Do you know your limitations?* they look at you with a blank stare" (105). I have found during my interview coaching that people will often fall into similar traps:

- **Memorizing a list of skills** (I am a good team player; I can work independently; I am a good problem solver; I can multi-task), but they don't know how to elaborate or link it to the job they are competing for.

- **Amazing skills but for the wrong job** (I am a great hockey player) and they use examples from this aspect of their life to answer every question. The problem is, by the end of the interview, they have proven why they should be drafted for a hockey team but not why they should be chosen for the job they are applying for!

- **Answer comes off negative.** In these instances, the candidate has answers and examples for the questions, but they actually demonstrate an inability rather than enhancing their abilities.

Let me give you an example:

I was approached by a talented and driven, young Black woman named Dianna who wanted some help preparing for a career in a traditionally male-dominated workforce. She already had some work experience in the field but was tainted by the fact that a colleague had openly told her "the only reason you are here is you are a diversity hire." This comment had angered her, and she was determined to show that she was as equally competent and deserving of the position as her white male counterparts. She had a strong desire to come across as **well-liked, competent,** and **respected** for her abilities. When we did her PI, we found that she was a **Guardian**—she was detail-oriented, steadfast, helpful, and diligent. She wanted to do things well and have time to ensure she didn't make an error. Although she loved being with people and socializing, she needed time to build trust and enjoyed her alone time to reflect and learn on her own. She enjoyed changing priorities but also wanted a stable working environment and the ability to learn a skill without constant changes. She was highly formal and enjoyed working with rules and structure. She tended to want to learn things and then do them well. She didn't want to have to delegate them to others. She tended to avoid conflict and might be seen to resist change if the idea seemed ambiguous or lacked clarity.

As we talked more about how she performed at work and what she was good at, an additional realization became apparent. In her desire to have people like her and see her as competent, she often tried to prove herself to them by taking on tasks independently and refusing help. As a woman, she wanted to show that she was physically capable of carrying all the tools on her own and didn't need to be accommodated. She thought she had been demonstrating that she was an effective team player: "I enjoy being part of a team and pulling my weight. I will identify a task that needs to be completed and I will ensure that I get it done well. I am not someone who relies on her teammates to carry her work. I think it is important to demonstrate that I have learned the skills and can do it on my own. I want them to know I am competent and a valued member of the team."

Unfortunately, in her last performance evaluation, the manager had shared that she rated low on teamwork. She was viewed by teammates as a bit of a lone wolf, someone who competed with others to get the job done and was not willing to accept help. It would appear that her desire to prove herself was impeding her ability to be seen as a team player. She was devastated and confused. How was she supposed to do both? What kind of example would she provide at her next interview when they asked about teamwork?

Turning a Negative into a Positive

I don't have to have done the job the candidate is applying for in order to help them improve their answers. I can read the job descriptions and do some research on what interviewers will be looking for. What I really focus on is *who* the people are that come to me, *why* they are applying for the job (needs and interests), and *how* I can help them better emphasize their strengths and demonstrate to the interviewer *why* they are their ideal candidate. They leave, think about their answers, and come back with much more confident and well-thought-out responses to the same questions.

Let's go back to Dianna for a second. You may be wondering how she improved her teamwork answer. The beauty of coaching is you do not have to provide the solutions, just the tools to get there. In fact, in this instance, all I really had to do was listen. She did the rest. In his book *The Coaching Habit: Say Less, Ask More and Change the Way You Lead Forever*, Michael Bungay Stanier tells us how to ask questions to help people learn and discover what they need to focus more on. In this instance, I asked Dianna to expand on her need to do things independently. When we had first started to work together, she had shared that she didn't want to ask me to help her unless I would let her pay me. I had laughingly refused, telling her she was a friend I was happy to help. Guess what I didn't do? I hadn't taken time to understand *why* she didn't feel comfortable asking for my help and how this tied into her teamwork answer. I could tell by her reaction. She wasn't swayed by my laughter. She still didn't want to accept my help. So I sat back and said, "tell me more." Dianna naturally expanded on her concerns. She said she had never felt comfortable asking for help from others. It wasn't because she was arrogant or thought she was better than other people. Instead, it was more due to her upbringing. From a young age, she had learned to be very self-reliant and non-codependent. She never wanted to be viewed as someone who took advantage of others or was overly needy. Those were not qualities she admired in others. Instead, she wanted to be able to demonstrate that she could learn the needed skills, apply herself, and if she needed help would always overcompensate the person giving it. "Your time is valuable," she said. "I don't want you to feel like I am using it up for free." I sat back and smiled. *This* is why I love coaching so much. Every time I work with a new person, I end up learning more from them than they do from me. I realized now that my initial response to her had been superficial and not met her needs. I tried again, "Dianna, thank you for sharing. Now I can better understand why you wanted to compensate me. Let me expand on why I coach. It's not for the money (at this point I had a well-paying corporate job and didn't see coaching as my full-time job). What I find fulfilling is having the opportunity to work with wonderful people and practice my skills. I learn as much from them as they do from me."

I went on to provide her with this insight: "By not allowing me to help you, I might think that you don't really value my expertise or that you think I am superficial and only doing it for the money." She was shocked. She hadn't taken into consideration how the other person might interpret her actions/words differently. We expanded this thinking to her teamwork answer and her performance review. If I were her teammate and she refused my help or advice, what might I think? Using this thought pattern allowed Dianna to self-reflect on how she approaches teamwork and how letting people help her could potentially meet the needs of others. Needless to say, we worked out a bartering system in which she could feel she was providing compensation for my services, and I got to help her grow and expand in her skills, experience, and interview answers.

When it came to how she answered that the next time, she learned to use language she had uncovered in her PI to better explain her intentions and thoughts. She was able to explain that her desire to do things well, and her eye for detail, contributed to a team setting. She explained her willingness to be helpful and take on some of the organizational tasks, allowing others to use their skills and strengths to seek out new options and do some of the more independent tasks. She was able to also provide a tangible example of just how she had used these skills in a team setting and now willingly relies on others to help her and mentor her with their strengths.

Applying These Strategies to Terri's Debrief

Let's go back to our scenario from Lesson 15. Terri has just joined you and Jill in a virtual debrief meeting. It is very apparent he is not feeling very motivated or supported. When you ask him to share his thoughts, he immediately starts talking about leaving the organization.

What are you going to say or do to inspire him to stay and remain motivated?

In my first years of human resources, I found these conversations to be very disjointed and non-productive. I tried to reassure the person that they could apply for the next job and gave them some tips on how to better prepare their responses, link their skills and experience to the applicable job description, and to practice them out loud to reduce nerves. I would often see the same person back in my office the next time and have to deliver similar news. What was I missing? They seemed equally confused and frustrated. In some cases, the person was actually doing the job and was just trying to win a full-time position. They should have been a "shoo-in" for the position, yet each time they would get beat out by less experienced, seemingly more confident members. That's when I realized my error. I was focusing only on what they needed to "do" and not "who" they were. Suddenly, when I started to introduce components of the PI assessment into our meetings, I saw the missing links emerging. Sometimes it was not what the person was saying, but why and how they were delivering it that impacted their interview. Remember, the interview panellists are *listening* to their responses. They are listening to not only the words used but also the way in which the situation is described and the confidence with which the person is saying it.

Let me give you an example to better illustrate this for Terri:

After you reviewed Terri's interview package and spoke to each of the three panelists, it emerged that he seemed to lack confidence in his responses. Panellists indicated he seemed to hesitate in providing examples and, even then, didn't explain what he had done in the situation. Instead, he kept saying, "we found a solution to the issue," "I spoke with my manager and they dealt with the issue," "my team and I work very effectively together and meet our deadlines." Given that Terri was applying for a supervisory position, the interviewers had been expecting answers that would help demonstrate how he led the team, used problem-solving skills to address issues, and had systems in place to address deadlines and the need to switch between tasks frequently.

Therefore, prior to the debrief session, you ask Terri to complete a PI assessment so that you can both learn more about *who* he is, what drives him, and identify his potential challenges. The results are very telling. Terri is an **Altruist**. He enjoys being supportive to others and finding harmony. He strives in his ability to collaborate, needs time to deliberate before making decisions that impact others, and is organized and precise. As you review this with him, you pay special attention to how these behaviours and traits may link to the responses he gave in his interview. You emphasize how his desire to collaborate and work cooperatively with others is a great quality; however, in his answers, he did not demonstrate how he would use these skills as a supervisor. For example, you decide to discuss his response to the question:

1. **As a supervisor, you will be expected to lead your team to meet required timelines and project goals. How have you demonstrated this skill in the past?**

In his response, he talked about working collaboratively with a team and meeting goals. But he didn't really outline for the panel how *he* would lead the team.

You need to emphasize the fact that just because he is a team player, it doesn't mean he can't also be an effective leader. You encourage him to tell you about leaders he admires and why. He points out traits in leaders that demonstrate the ability to empower others, help when there is a deadline crunch, listen to the members, and ask for insight. After all, *we admire in others what we admire in ourselves.* Now you can coach him on how to use his assets to better explain how he will lead the team to ensure they meet their goals and deadlines.

This same approach can be used when reviewing his answers to other interview questions.

2. **Tell us about a time you were challenged with completing a difficult task and what steps you took to accomplish it.**

Again, Terri emphasized the fact he likes multi-tasking, can effectively juggle tasks and remain organized. However, because he is slightly more risk averse, he would prefer to ensure the answers are found collaboratively rather than coming up with the answers on his own. It only makes sense that when he answered this question, he used a lot of "we" statements rather than "I."

You will need to encourage Terri to really think about what *he* does to contribute to the problem-solving tasks. Maybe it is ensuring that the group doesn't just jump to conclusions or go with the first idea. Because he excels in collaboration, he can help to ensure that everyone is heard and all ideas are brought forward. He builds harmony on the team and, as a result, a better and more well-developed answer to the problem is found. Teaching people to use language found in the PI often gives them the ability to better explain why and how they do things. For the interviewer, this provides a much deeper insight into who they are and how they will perform in the role. It is a win/win.

Now to the next question:

3. **Please tell us about a time in which you had a conflict with another member and what you did to resolve this issue.**

Here you will be able to identify ways to help assist Terri in his own professional development needed for the role of supervisor. Terri is not a *take charge* kind of person. It would never occur to him to say that he dealt with the issue without consulting someone. He is cautionary in making decisions and may not be seen by some as strategic enough.

Armed with this information, you can help to give Terri opportunities to potentially work in an acting supervisory role or as a coach. This will help him to build confidence that he does have the knowledge and skills to hold people accountable and yet can find ways to do so in a non-authoritative way. In fact, you can show him Lesson 4 of this book to expose him to additional learning he can do on leadership styles and assist him in developing a style of leadership he is comfortable with.

Creating Opportunities for Growth

By using this process, you can also ensure you are meeting Terri's needs for **validation** and **financial security**. You are providing him with tangible examples of how he can be a very effective supervisor and how he can ensure he will "rock his next interview." You are building trust and respect with an employee, and you are supporting professional development. If we go back to *First, Break All the Rules,* you are once again meeting the needs of the following two elements.

Element 11 — In the last six months, someone at work has talked to me about my progress.

Element 12 — This last year, I have had opportunities at work to learn and grow.

You are talking to someone about their progress in a very real and useful way. You are providing them with opportunities to learn and grow. You have used both an empathetic approach as well as an objective/factual detailed approach to outline your response and discussion. You have also mentored Jan in learning a more advanced approach in providing useful feedback to a member.

PART 5

—

INSPIRING ORGANIZATIONAL GROWTH

LESSON 17

Knowledge Builds Understanding

Is Your Workplace Inclusive?

What is your definition of the word **diversity**? What does it mean to want to have an **inclusive** workforce? What do **equitable** practices look like?

When it comes to how I define **diversity**, it is influenced by my own experiences and knowledge. Your definition may be different. Both are, I believe, right. The purpose of this exercise is to get you to think about how creating diverse, inclusive, and equitable workplaces require all of us to be vulnerable, openly demonstrate a willingness to work with people different from ourselves, and recognize that we each carry with us our own conscious or unconscious biases. Just as we have learned in other lessons, this can both challenge and enrich our experiences as leaders.

I define **diversity** in a very broad spectrum to include socioeconomic background, culture, ethnicity, religion/creed, sexual orientation, gender identity, race, ability, age, and citizenship. I view it as a beautiful blend of everything that makes up a person and how they are uniquely different from others. I also think it is very important to recognize and acknowledge that many aspects of diversity are cross-sectional and linked. An elderly Black female who lives in poverty will unfortunately be exposed to various aspects of discrimination and health issues. This may result in her having additional issues with mental health and physical health. The issues are rarely isolated to only one concern or aspect. Yet no two people have the same experiences; therefore, we need to caution ourselves from grouping people into "diversity identities" and making biased assumptions about what they may face.

I define an **inclusive workplace** as one that values the unique differences of its members, makes a genuine and progressive effort to develop awareness and understanding, and instillssubstantive changes to its policies, training, and practices to remove barriers and address biases. It is an organization that hears its members and addresses their concerns. It is focused on ensuring people are both physically and psychologically safe and enables them to bring their authentic self to work and thrive in their environment.

I define **equitable practices** as those that allow everyone to start from an equal starting point. This may mean, in some cases, you need to adjust the starting line. Many find this concept challenging and uncomfortable. However, I will challenge you to look at it like this: Not everyone has had the same past, same opportunities, same health, same rights. Equity means we take those things into consideration. It allows us, as leaders, to recognize and acknowledge inequity and give people opportunities to shine and compete for positions and opportunities. It helps our organizations grow.

Bringing Your Authentic Self to Work

This idea is brought to life in a TED Talk by Jodi-Ann Burey called *"The Myth of Bringing Your Authentic Self to Work."* She explains that as a Black woman doing diversity outreach work for organizations, she was often told, "we are so excited to have you here, to hear your perspectives." However, when she tried to be her authentic self, expressing her thoughts, asking questions, and providing insights into biases that existed in the organization, she was quickly relabelled as a threat and told she would need to conform to the existing organizational culture. Therefore, it is clear that organizations need to *first* do genuine and challenging work with their leaders and employees to expand how they define and understand the value of diversity and how they approach hiring and internal practices to create inclusivity. Too often, employees like Jodi-Ann and Dianna (in our previous lesson) are subjected to opinions that they are "just a diversity hire." Allowing this type of verbiage, labelling, and assumption building to exist only perpetuates the marginalization and oppression of these employees. Leaders must develop ways to ensure that all members feel welcomed and safe in their organizations. Much of this work starts with learning *how* the diversity that this person brings with them, through their own lived experience, can enhance the organization. The next step is then to learn how you as a leader can mobilize their new opinions, ideas, knowledge, and experience into existing processes. Unfortunately, change of any kind can be viewed as threatening or negative. Being open to people and approaches that are different from our own is often difficult. As we have discussed in previous lessons, ego, vulnerability, needs, and leadership styles will all come into play. However, we have also learned that the willingness to be vulnerable and learn more about yourself can help you become more open and comfortable with learning more about others. Therefore, as a leader, if you have already done the necessary work to approach these situations with an open and curious mind, then you will be better equipped to identify and address barriers and biases as they arise. You will have the ability to create safe spaces, support open dialogue, and, by *knowing* your employees, ensure that a trusting and safe relationship begins to develop.

Previous Training Can Be a Guide

We can learn a lot from previous training that can be applied to our work environments. I am sure you have taken many fantastic and riveting leadership courses designed to increase your knowledge and understanding of diverse communities and the issues that impact them. Courses I have taken include: Indigenous cultural awareness, anti-black racism, transgender and LGBTQ2SIA+ awareness, creating equity for disability and ability communities, gender equity seminars, newcomer inclusion webinars designed to improve HR practices, and many more. With each course, I learn new things, meet fabulous people, and become even more aware of the potential barriers that are present in hiring, retaining, and promoting employees, and how they impede the ability to foster an inclusive workplace. Never has it been more apparent than now that we need to get to know *who* our previously excluded or marginalized members are, what struggles they are presented with, and how we can improve our processes if we want to be truly considered inclusive workforces.

In their fabulous book *The Leader's Guide to Unconscious Bias,* authors Pamela Fuller, Mark Murphy, and Anne Chow highlight some very practical and powerful ways leaders can challenge themselves to create high-performing teams. They introduce the concept that "bias can inhibit decision making, performance, innovation, and results in a workplace. Employees who perceive themselves as the target of bias are three times more likely to withhold ideas, be disengaged, and leave within a year" (13).

In Lesson 8, we explored the question:

What type of person would fit the mould for your ideal candidate?

When you think of your ideal candidate, think about the people you enjoy working with the most.

- Are you thinking entirely about skills and experience, or are you also focusing on personality and behaviours?

Now also add into this equation the aspect(s) of diversity as I have defined them. Are your decisions consciously or unconsciously biased as you also take these factors into consideration?

Has your organization traditionally hired persons from similar diverse (non-diverse) backgrounds?

- Is your organization representative of your community?
- Would an increased knowledge of *who* your employees are, and what diverse aspects they bring with them, enhance your ability to offer them new opportunities and retain them within your organization?
- Does your organization have equitable hiring, promotional, and training practices that allow all members an equal chance to advance? How will you answer this question?

Fuller, Murphy, and Chow further explain that our identity, who we are, and how we think and approach the world are based on many things, including: **information** we read, hear, and watch; our **education**; the **context** in which we live, practice our beliefs, and function; the **culture** we are exposed to (race, religion, ethnicity, geography); our **innate traits** (similar to the behavioural traits found in our PI); and our **experiences** (21–22). These factors impact how we experience the world and how we interact with it.

Acknowledge Your Own Privilege

I want to first acknowledge my awareness that what I write and share in these next few lessons does come from a place of white, middle income, cisgender, female privilege. I do not have the same lived experiences nor have I been presented with some of the barriers and biases that have been imposed on others. I do, however, want to be an ally. Someone who is willing to learn, admits to their errors, strives to build trust, and is held accountable. Someone who invests time, love, and effort into creating and supporting inclusive efforts. I recognize that being an ally is not self-declared. You must earn that designation and be consistent in your actions. As leaders, we need to be openly engaged in the learning and understanding of how we and our organizations have erred in the past. We need to both study and apply this learning in meaningful, intentional, and effective ways. We need to be not merely transactional in our actions but transformational. Sometimes we will fail. The key is to admit to our errors and start again.

My Challenge to You

My challenge to you in Lesson 17 is this: start from a place of growth. A desire to learn more, challenge your assumptions, and re-examine how and why things are done. I want to empower you, if you haven't already, to engage in new learning on your own: read books, attend conferences, and explore the social issues that are impacting our world today, including reconciliation with Indigenous communities, Black Lives Matter, hate crimes against religious groups and those identifying as transgender or LGBTQ2SIA+, the socioeconomic struggles that many of our new, well-educated, experienced immigrants face when seeking employment in Canada, the challenges faced by those with mental health issues in retaining and maintaining employment, and more. As you develop a keen understanding for the issues and struggles that many in society face—and subsequently the impact on some of your employees—the more you will be able to gain their *trust* and have real discussions on how to improve their experience in your organization. For my part, I will help to illustrate how getting to know your employees includes understanding how these aspects impact their lives, their education, their ability to get the necessary work experience, their desire to remain in your organization, and some of the challenges they face. I will share lessons I have learned and mistakes I have made. I will introduce you to some fantastic teachers and potentially reignite your interest to learn even more.

Let's start here, with a few statistics that will hopefully touch your heart and engage your learning:

Did You Know?

1. By the time Canadians reach forty years of age, one in two have or have had a mental illness (Centre for Addiction and Mental Health-Driving Change).

2. Forty-five percent of transgender and non-binary Canadians have been harassed at work or school (Trans PULSE Canada).

3. The number of hate crimes based on race or ethnicity committed in Canada grew 37% from 2019 to 2020. (The Daily Canada).

4. Thousands of unmarked graves have been located at residential school sites in Canada—further searches for unmarked graves at other sites are ongoing. (Deer)

5. Nearly five million Canadians (that's one in every seven individuals) are living below the poverty line ("Poverty in Canada").

6. Due to limited pensions and low retirement savings, it is estimated that one in four Canadians between the ages of

sixty-five and seventy are still employed (The Daily-Labour Force Survey- Canada).

Knowledge Builds Understanding

I believe that having knowledge builds understanding. Re-examine the facts you just read. Do you think any of these facts may be impacting your employees and your workforce? By knowing these facts and more, could you potentially increase the inclusive and equitable nature of your organization? This might include the creation of flexible schedules, accommodations, sensitivity training, new policies and procedures, and even new job roles that might better meet the needs of future and current employees. However, in order to do so, you will first need to learn what barriers exist and who may be facing them. Then you will be able to apply understanding and empathy to their situation. Just as we discussed in Lesson 15, your role will be to truly listen, hear their concerns, and then work together to find solutions.

Do You Know What Issues Your Employees Face?

In their book *The Leader's Guide to Unconscious Bias,* authors Pamela Fuller, Mark Murphy, and Anne Chow highlight that "organizations and leaders are responsible for setting the conditions for belonging" (83). To do this effectively, you need to know what issues your employees are facing and then include them in developing effective solutions.

Over the years, I have watched as well-intentioned organizations approached this process incorrectly and ended up reinforcing an "us and them" atmosphere of mistrust and frustration. This lesson was powerfully and best explained by Aiko Bethea, an expert in diversity, inclusion, and equity in her podcast interview with Brené Brown. In the *Dare to Lead* podcast episode, entitled *"Creating Transformative Culture"*, Bethea shares that "diversity, equity, inclusion and belonging work can not be transactional. It has to be relational if it is going to transformational. This work should not be reactional. Although it is urgent to do this work, leaders often fall victim to action bias. You need to have intentionality. You need to give it the high value it deserves. It has to be strategic, intentional, and not just done with urgency. You need to ensure your members feel safe, included and not retraumatized by the work. Make sure you are talking about equity and holding people and processes accountable. You want to ensure you methods are well thought out so that they don't cause further fracturing."

We need to take the time, involve people who can guide and teach us, *always* be willing to admit to our errors, and hold ourselves accountable. This will result in truly transformational work that builds trust, enables relationships, and remains consistent.

Let's Do a Survey!

Often organizations will start their learning process by attempting to gather data on *who* their members are. However, most organizations, when asked to provide their diversity statistics, struggle to be able to provide accurate answers. Therefore, many have introduced the use of surveys to try and better understand who has joined their organization and who has left. Surveys are focused on trying to find answers to questions like:

1. How many employees do you have that belong to specifically identified groups?
2. What is the cultural representation found within your organization?
3. How many languages do your employees speak, read, write?
4. What is the gender discrepancy in your organizational positions?
5. How many of your employees have an identified disability?
6. How many of your leaders belong to specifically identified groups?
7. How long do you retain employees from specifically identified groups?
8. Why did they leave your organization?

Would you be able to pull these statistics right now? HR may or may not have some of the answers. Respecting employees' right to privacy on their personal information, many HR branches refrain from asking questions that do not pertain to the job requirements. Remember Zack from Lesson 8? He was hired to work on the production line at an online distribution company. He fills orders as they come in and sends them to shipping. Nowhere in his application was he required to disclose that he speaks five languages, is of Romanian descent, and has been diagnosed with partial hearing loss. Therefore, the only information HR currently has is his age, gender, citizenship, and education level. He wouldn't even show up in your needed statistical responses.

Organizations, recognizing that they are unable to provide needed data, therefore often provide candidates with voluntary diversity forms they can complete at the time of application or hire. In it they are given the opportunity to disclose diverse aspects of their background and how they identify. I have received mixed reviews and concerns from members and candidates on this type of survey. While some celebrate the idea of being able to indicate they are part of a specific community or culture, others remain cautious and concerned about how the information might be used or considered.

Therefore, some organizations have opted for an anonymous type of survey, in which the needed data can be collected but the member's identity remains protected. While this answers some concerns, it limits the ability for the organization to respond to most of the questions that ask for specific diversity numbers. How many members outside of mainstream candidates you have in specific job roles and how effectively they are moving up in your organization remains unanswered. Equally concerning is the fact that they are also unable to determine if these members have left the organization and why.

In her *Open Letter to Corporate America,* Aiko Bethea also cautions organizations from "limiting their metrics to demographic representation and counting numbers of ethnic groups gender, abilities, etc. We need to caution ourselves from clumping groups together and assuming all members of a group have the same experience. A Black woman's experience is different than that of an Asian or Latino employee. You should be able to clearly discern the different experience between a white woman and women of other ethic groups."

Regardless of how you approach it, people will only fill out the survey and provide you with the information you need if they *trust* the information is going to be used objectively and is designed to actually create change rather that just check a box on an annual report.

Building Trust FIRST

In Lesson 11, we discussed that trust is linked to many core values of honesty, respect, loyalty, commitment, and integrity. Therefore, trust is not something that many people will give easily. It is one of those fundamental things that is difficult to gain and easy to lose. It also plays a very key role in the leadership of diverse members of our organizations. In many cases, we need to *rebuild* trust with members of populations who have experienced marginalization or oppression, who—due to the biases and hatred of others—have experienced many situations in which trust was broken or abused. We need to make a concerted effort to understand all employees' cultural or lived experience and acknowledge that trust will not be regained easily. In many cases, we will have to do a lot of personal work on our own conscious or unconscious biases before we can ask anyone to trust us. We may need to look at how we have downplayed or hidden aspects of our own lives and identities in our professional life. By taking this step, we will be able to better relate to how demoralizing it must be for some employees to have to hide portions of their life in order to protect themselves from negative opinions, labels, and actions. We will need to acknowledge when we make mistakes, activate triggers, use microaggressions, and display a lack of understanding. It will require us, as leaders, to model the willingness to be vulnerable and act without ego in our leadership journey.

In Lessons 18 and 19, we will explore how applying much of the learning found in this book can help us begin to lead our organizations in inclusive thoughts and practices.

LESSON 18

Small Changes Can Have a Significant Impact

Knowledge Creates Inclusive Possibilities

Sometimes our best lessons are learned after we blunder. I have learned that the key is to: develop an awareness and realization for when you blunder and have the humility to admit it, the fortitude to apologize for your biases, and the willingness to learn how to correct your errors. Learning about and developing an appreciation for people who are different from ourselves doesn't happen instantly. We have all grown up with our own stories, our own assumptions, biases, and opinions. The first step in change requires that you rid yourself of ego so that you are able to be vulnerable and humble enough to see the world from a new angle. The more you spend time with those that you *define* as different from yourself, the more you understand their experiences and the inequalities they have faced, see similarities, and develop admiration for each other. In fact, as we have learned in this book, acceptance and appreciation for how others can contribute and enrich our lives will inevitably make us better leaders.

My Learning Journey

I have had the pleasure and opportunity to work with and lead a diverse group of people over the years. The beauty of this statement is that in the beginning I often had no idea just how multifaceted my colleagues' lives were. I didn't ask colleagues to disclose; instead, through my actions, I showed them they could *trust* me to share more about their lives. In doing so, I have been able to further identify and recognize some of my own unconscious biases and learn from them. In *The Leader's Guide to Unconscious Bias,* the authors explain that "Only when I cultivate meaningful connections can I see past bias and value the people around me" (74).

Let me give you an example:

Aadav was an HR co-op student. He had already completed his undergraduate degree in India, had an impressive resume, and now had enrolled in a post-graduate degree in HR in Canada. He was soft-spoken and pleasant to work with. He came in every day, worked hard, and then rushed out the door to his next job. He would rarely take a break, and I had to encourage him to stop and eat. I didn't know much about him. He sometimes asked to work through his break so that he could leave a half-hour early at 3:30 p.m. Sometimes during lunch, I would see that he was on his phone and appeared to be speaking to someone in his native language, Hindi. One day, I took him for a drive to pick up some documents we needed. During the drive, we started to talk about family, and I shared stories about my kids. What Aadav shared shocked me. He talked about his aunt and uncle who had helped to raise him. They lived on a small farm with a very limited income in India, and his small cousin had recently fallen ill and needed hospitalization. Money, he explained, was very tight, so he had been sending money home for her medical expenses. When I asked how he was able to find the money to help, he told me that in addition to his forty-hour "free co-op placement," he also worked from 4:00 p.m. to 10:00 p.m. three days a week at a second job, and then about fifteen hours at a third job on the weekends. He said he would work more, but his work visa prohibited him from working more than forty hours a week. Suddenly I understood his need to leave his co-op position at 3:30 p.m. on specific days. He needed to get to work. I also understood why he often seemed to have very little food. He was sending money home for his cousin and paying rent, tuition debt, cell phone bills, and for public transportation. There wasn't much left for food.

Armed with this new information, I brought in extra vegetarian food to "share" with the office staff at lunch. I made sure Aadav was able to take breaks *and* leave at 3:30 p.m. on the days he had to work. I checked in with him about the progress of his cousin's health. As a result, when his eight-week co-op placement was done, he asked if he could stay in touch with me. Over the years he would drop by the office, check in and share news of his marriage and job prospects. Five years later, he still says working for our organization was his best work experience so far, and he hopes to someday work in a similar workplace.

As a leader, meeting Aadav helped me alter my perspective and understanding of my diverse groups of new co-op students. First, I learned that earning the HR postgraduate certificate was common for many international students in Canada. The co-op portion of the course enabled them to get the necessary work experience in a Canadian setting. Secondly, I learned that many of the family, financial, and cultural issues and stressors international students faced were very different from my own. I hadn't grown up in a family where children were expected to be financially responsible for parents and extended family members. I had grown up in a family of privilege and economic stability. Learning how hard Aadav was working to try and support family and develop needed skills to get a better paying job in Canada impressed me. It enabled me to become more conscious of the needs of my future employees and how I had initially failed Aadav. I needed to ensure that I paid attention to each of my employees. Did they seem stressed after they got off the phone with their family? Did they need fifteen minutes to take a quick call and deal with issues at hand? Did they need to leave early to take an elderly parent to an appointment or help a friend? By recognizing your employees as a diverse group of individuals, all with their own lives, backgrounds, issues, and concerns, you can start to have this conversation and learn more about how you can make their experiences equitable and inclusive.

Are We Creating Barriers?

I don't want readers to approach this lesson and assume that I am suggesting only quick, Band-Aid type approaches to creating equity and inclusion. Yes, we do need to ensure that each member we meet is treated as an individual and ensure their needs are met to the best of our ability at the time. However, I want to also challenge you to think much deeper and critically when it comes to how our organizations are potentially enabling and perpetuating economic barriers for new employees. An example of this may be found in the continued utilization of free internships, co-operative positions, grant-funded positions, and volunteer workers. In *The Globe and Mail*, author Uday Rana discusses the growing economic barriers being created by these types of positions that bring important issues to light. I have utilized these issues and others to create three situations through which leaders can broach this topic of economic barriers and start to challenge their own thinking.

The first situation involves new immigrants who arrive in Canada with previous experience in their given field of medicine, trades, engineering, nursing, teaching, accounting, and so on, yet due to different rules and regulations are often required to attain Canadian *licensing or experience* in the field. This may result in them returning to school and choosing a program that will enable them to participate in a "free internship or co-op," allowing them to gain the needed experience and knowledge prior to writing for their licence. In these cases, people are forced to do what Aadav did and work multiple jobs while also trying to complete a free internship. In other cases, new immigrants find themselves unable to afford to "work for free" and therefore are forced to stay in low-paying jobs not related to their previous field of study or experience. This may ultimately impact their ability to gain their permanent residency. Although recent changes in Ontario have started to reduce the need for additional Canadian licensing, many barriers still exist. Hiring and recruitment practices are still looking for experienced workers. Organizations will need to ensure that their HR branches and hiring managers are open to considering experience the person has attained in a different country other than Canada. This will enable the hiring process to become more equitable and attainable for members such at Aadav.

The second situation is created by employers who value previous *volunteer work* as an asset they favour in new applicants. Let me give you an example. As an employer, you value community involvement and therefore look for applicants who have generously given of their time to their community in a volunteer capacity. After all, this action of volunteerism exemplifies an altruist mindset, a willingness to help others, a willingness to think beyond yourself and meet the needs of others. All great, right? Yes, but unfortunately, not everyone can afford to take ten to forty hours out of their month to do *free* work. I would often see this in new applicants. Some had their education paid for, lived at home, and were able to take time off from a paid position to volunteer and give back to their community. However, others had been single parents, paid for their own schooling, rent, food, and worked more than forty hours every week to make ends meet while also ensuring they passed their courses and effectively parented their child. They didn't have the time, wealth, or energy to also do *free* work. Did this make them any less committed, altruistic, or dedicated to helping others? No. If anything, they were demonstrating their ability to handle stress, multi-task, prioritize, and handle finances! Therefore, as leaders we need to rethink what we are placing value on and how we seek to have applicants demonstrate it. Instead of asking for volunteer work, the interview could simply contain a question on the importance of helping others and ask the applicant to describe how they demonstrate this quality. This will broaden the possible ways to answer the question and enable the interviewer to have a better opportunity to learn about the resilience of some of their applicants in the face of adversity.

The third situation involves employers utilizing *free* or *low-paying* employment opportunities to fulfill needed job assignments. Although many such systems were originally designed with the intent to provide people with job experience and mentoring opportunities in a field of interest, it is now apparent that they have created a hierarchy within applicants. Let me give you an example. Employers often apply for and utilize government grants, or free university or college interns, to try and fill temporary job assignments. After all, it's a win-win, right? The employer gets some needed work or project completed, it doesn't have to come out of the budget, and the applicant gets some needed experience in their field of choice. The reality, however, is that an applicant often has to work in multiple jobs so they can *afford* to take the low- or non-paying position. Many organizations are now rethinking this systemic barrier they are creating and realizing that it does not align with their mission and vision to be an inclusive and barrier-free employer. Therefore, as leaders, we need to consider whether saving a little money should be our priority in these situations. Instead, organizations should value the opportunity to bring new, creative, and innovative minds into their workplace, even if only for short projects or assignments, and offer additional compensation or wages for the position. This, in turn, will assist in the removal of economic barriers that face many applicants seeking to gain needed experience.

Initiating Change

As Bethea reminds us in her podcast discussion with Brené Brown, it is imperative that we don't jump to solution-based thinking when it comes to addressing issues of diversity and inclusion. Well-intentioned organizations often will form internal equity, diversity, and inclusion committees to try and address their internal processes that may be impeding the attraction or retention of new employees from diverse communities. Invitations are sent out to the existing employees to join a work group designed to identify existing barriers. However, often only a small representative group comes forward. Being part of a working group can be even more threatening than being asked to fill out a survey. In a group setting, you are hoping people will openly share and disclose personal experiences. As we have learned, learning styles, needs and behaviours, triggers and personal biases will also impact someone's willingness to participate. Therefore, in order to truly get diverse input, you will need to diversify the methods and sources of your input. You will need to consult with those both inside and out of your organization. You will need to ensure that participants are given the opportunity to provide their feedback and ideas through a variety of methods (by email, anonymous suggestion boxes, one-on-one meetings, and group settings). You will also need to incorporate some of the inclusive team-building activities found in Lessons 10, 11, and 12 to ensure that committee members are aware of each other's behaviours, needs, triggers, and learning styles. Taking time to create an inclusive foundation will help to ensure you gain the needed insight.

Learning from Your Community

In 2010, I had the extreme pleasure to work with members of our transgender community. Admittedly, I had very little previous understanding of the issues that faced our trans community, but an opportunity for learning presented itself, and I took it. It started with just an introductory conversation and an agreement to review some of current policies to ensure that they were not inadvertently discriminating against or limiting the career trajectories of the transgender community in any of our practices. It turned out we were.

One of the first transgender community members I met, Phil, was young, vivacious, a fantastic speaker, and easily liked. He held a university degree and seemed like he would be an ideal employee for an organization to hire. Yet he was unemployed. He shared the struggles he was having in gaining employment. Organizations required him to provide a copy of his degree as proof of education with his application. His concern centred on the fact that the degree was in his legal birth name (the name he was given when he was assigned female at birth). Therefore, by providing his degree to a potential employer, he was "outing" himself as a transgender person before they had even met him. Remember the statistic that 45% of transgender and non-binary Canadians have been harassed at work or school? Phil had already experienced this firsthand. Previous employers had forced him to wear a name tag with his birth name (sometimes called a dead name), even though he identified as male and had chosen the name Phil. There had been no legal reason for forcing him to wear such a name tag. The manager had just been biased in their beliefs that Phil shouldn't be allowed to use a male name at work because it was not his legal name. The result had been customers constantly asking about his name tag and misgendering him. Customers would question Phil on the fact that he appeared male but was wearing a female name tag. Imagine just trying to do your job, and each time you serve a customer they ask about your *gender identity*! It was cruel and unnecessary and just further encouraged abuse and bias.

I was horrified by Phil's story. As I was introduced to other members of the transgender community, I learned that their stories and experiences were both similar and strikingly unique, whether young or old. Some had had successful careers but had been forced to hide their authentic selves from bosses, fellow employees, and even family. They shared their frustration, concern, and ultimate fear of being "found out." Others had attempted to "come out" at school and with family only to be shunned and rejected. They had found themselves forced to make decisions about how *authentic* they could afford to be. Imagine having to live your life as someone else, someone society wants you to be, and never being able to share your true feelings and authentic self with others? Imagine the stress, the self-doubt, the depression this would cause? Sadly, statistics tell us that 45% of the those identifying as transgender have attempted suicide at least once in their lifetime ("Trans PULSE Canada").

Small Changes Matter

Sometimes it is the small changes we make that can have the greatest impact. Let me give you a small example of what an organization can do to rid itself of biased practices you may not even be aware of. Many in the transgender community have shared their fear of "willfully outing themselves to an employer." This often occurs on an application, as Phil previously explained.

Pull out one of your own employment applications. How is it worded?

1. Does it read "given name" or "legal name?" This can easily be changed to "name" or "preferred name." In most cases, the person's legal birth name is not needed until they are already hired, and only if you need it for a legal purpose (tax forms, criminal clearance).

2. Do you ask for gender on your application? Why? If there is no *bona fide* reason related to the position/job, remove it.

3. Do you ask for proof of education initially with the application? Can it be moved to the background stage? By this time, hopefully, you will have established some trust with the candidate and they may feel safer disclosing the documentation if it is in their legal, birth-gender name. Additionally, an HR manager would be able to

safeguard the information and have it disclosed only to the people that required it.

I have continued to work with and be an ally for the transgender community ever since. I am still very close friends with many I met through this process. Phil has gone on to be a successful advocate, trainer, and speaker for the community and is gainfully employed in a job he loves—helping trans youth find their place in society. Together we design training material and speak at events to increase the awareness and understanding of the transgender community.[9]

Although I could share with you many more experiences of how building trust and learning about diverse community members has helped me enrich the person that I am and how I choose to lead, I think *you* should also have time to reflect on your own experiences. Think about those you have led.

- What aspects of their diversity are you aware of that perhaps you didn't know initially?

- How did you gain this knowledge?

- How has it assisted you or maybe hampered you in your ability to lead and understand them?

- What could your organization do differently?

- Is there more you need to learn?

I encourage everyone to do this needed work, from hockey and sports coaches to volunteer leaders, and to bosses in large corporations. We all need to understand how making small changes can literally save lives. Being part of an inclusive team or work environment can be life-altering for people. You may be the first group that has ever accepted them for who they are. Imagine what that can do for someone's self-esteem and self-confidence. Imagine also how this can enhance your organization.

---

9   If you would like to learn more, please visit https://egale.ca, a support group created to increase understanding for this community.

Mental Health Challenges

By the time Canadians reach forty years of age, one in two have or have had a mental illness. The Centre for Addiction and Mental Health (CAMH) defines the term "mental illness" as a wide range of disorders that impact the mood, thinking, and behaviour of a person. Examples include but are not limited to depression, anxiety, schizophrenia, mood disorders, and more. The illness can be associated with distress and/or impairment of functioning, with symptoms varying from mild to severe. Mental health can also be linked to addictions, such as alcoholism and gambling, that people use to attempt to deal with symptoms. Additionally, mental and physical health are often linked. People with long-term medical conditions are much more likely to also experience mood disorders. Conversely, people who have mood disorders are much more prone to developing medical conditions due to the impact stress has on the body.

It is fair to say that some of your employees suffer from mental illness. Yet very few are going to be willing to initially disclose this information to you. Stigma around mental health, and the fear that it may cause an employee to lose their job or be denied a promotion, is very real. People try to hide mental health issues and, given that it is not a visible difference, they will likely succeed. Unfortunately, mental health issues often impact the employee's ability to work consistent hours and impacts their attendance. Supervisors may be coming to you frustrated with employees who seem to be always booking off sick, coming in late, and have inconsistent attendance. When it comes time to recommend an employee for a full-time position or one that has more responsibility, this same employee will be overlooked because they are viewed as unreliable. Yet that same employee may be the hardest working member of the team. When they are healthy and feeling well, they come to work and contribute to the success of the group.

I have been honoured to be able to sit with some of these employees (sadly this normally occurs during an attendance review meeting) and have them share their struggles with me. I have learned so much about what it means to try to function with a mental illness, how anxiety and panic attacks literally consume them, how depression can keep them in bed for days unable to respond to text messages and emails from inquiring bosses, how medications designed to regulate their moods also make them sleepy and unable to rise for that morning alarm clock. I have learned about the need to create flexible schedules and adjust start times to meet the needs of these employees. I have encouraged members to get necessary treatment and counselling to aid them in dealing with some of their stressors. I have watched while these same employees regain their self-confidence and belief that they are a valued part of the organization.

Remember in Lessons 10 and 11 when we touched on getting to know the core needs and interests of your employees? As you explore the issues of diversity and both the challenges and opportunities it may present for you and your employees, remember to think about the root issues. What are their core needs?

- **Aadav's** needs were focused on **financial security** and **family health**.

- **Phil** needed to be his **authentic self**, the ability to **gain financial security** and **recognition for his abilities**.

- For those suffering from mental illness, the needs identified to me were **financial security** but also to **feel valued and respected** by the organization.

Being an Ally

In *The Leader's Guide to Unconscious Bias,* authors Pamela Fuller, Mark Murphy, and Anne Chow remind us that "being an ally is a verb not a noun. It is defined by your actions. Understanding others' experiences and offering support can make a world of difference with issues. Allies understand that addressing unconscious bias is critical to morale and business imperatives, especially when they are in a position of relative power compared to those on the receiving end of the bias" (175).

In every case, people need to feel safe and secure in their work environment, free of discrimination, shaming, blaming, and biases. The best thing you can do is to *ask* those who are impacted how you can help. If you don't know *who* they are, then start by building trust or re-building trust, so they will tell you. Your goal should be to enable those in your workplace, and who wish to join your workplace, to feel like they belong. True belonging, as defined by Brené Brown in *Braving the Wilderness,* does not require you to change who you are; it requires you to be who you are. We owe it to the people we choose to lead to ensure they can share with us their authentic selves. Being forced to pretend or hide parts of oneself is not something anyone should have to endure.

Call to Action

After reading these last two lessons, what tangible actions do you want to take?

- What do you know?

- What do you need to learn?

- How can you use this information to do some of the work Aiko Bethea challenges us, as leaders, to do?

LESSON 19

Sometimes You Are Missing Critical Information

The Risk of Making Assumptions

Remember growing up as a kid and attending those family events? Someone, a well-meaning auntie or nosy cousin, would inevitably ask, "So what do you want to be when you grow up?" How many of you cringed at the question? Were you also acutely aware that depending on how you answered their question you would get a well-meaning nod or a look of shocked concern? The effects of societal expectations can continue on in life and affect how employees consider their own capacity for advancement. They can also affect what we think of potential candidates or those asking for information and expressing interest in entering our field.

Societal Expectations

Society has placed a lot of status and expectation on how you answered that question. If you replied doctor, teacher, lawyer, architect, engineer, you were more likely to receive smiling nods. These were positions of status and represented financial security. Did you anticipate the same reaction if you replied, "freelance writer, painter, hockey player, or movie star?" Maybe not.

How your auntie reacted depended on her biases and assumptions. If you were male and replied "nurse," did she look at you sceptically? Did she think males couldn't be nurses, or did she consider a nurse *less than* that of a doctor or surgeon?

If you replied "painter" and you came from a family that celebrated the arts and creativity, you might have received smiles and nodding approval.

If you replied "engineer," but your current social status did not equate to someone who would have the financial backing for such an elaborate education, you may have received comments like, "You are daydreaming. You need to find yourself a job!"

If your answer was the desire to be an "architect" but teachers had labelled you as lazy and distracted in school, and your high school marks were barely meeting a passing grade, did your guidance counsellor automatically assume you couldn't possibly go to university?

If you excitedly announced the desire to be a "writer" but you came from a cultural background in which the firstborn was expected to achieve great things and financially support their parents, this answer would likely have received a hard "No!"

Assessing Applicants

We need to apply this thinking to how we assess our own candidates and their applications to work for us. This is important information to keep in mind as you are posting ads for new employees and reviewing resumes. Are you making assumptions about whether they are suited for the job based on their resume, their education, and their interests? Let me give you a few examples:

Abdoul has always wanted to be a doctor. He has dreamed about it, watched all the medical shows growing up—like *Grey's Anatomy*, *Bones*, and *House*—to learn the terminology and as much as possible about cases he might someday work on. He finished high school and enrolled in a couple of night classes at his local university. During the day and on weekends, he works security and as a maintenance person in your building. You have bumped into him a few times, and today you strike up a conversation as you both ride the elevator to the tenth floor. "So Abdoul," you ask, "how are your night classes going? What are you studying?" He replies, "I am taking a lab technician course, but I hope to be a doctor one day." What is your gut reaction? What questions come to mind? What assumptions are you making? *(It's okay, only you know what you are thinking, so feel free to be honest.)*

I have been in a similar situation to this, and I will tell you my gut reaction. I was initially concerned and saddened by what I presumed was his reality. Here he was, working hard, earning minimum wage, and only taking a couple of night classes. At this rate he would be thirty years old before he even finished his undergrad. His work experience wasn't really going to help him have a competitive medical school application. They wanted community work and experience in a medically related field. How was he going to find time to do that? I saw his aspirations to be a doctor as fictional and stargazing. I didn't think he would make it. But he did. You see, I got my assumptions wrong. He had gotten the security job so that he could apply for a position at the hospital. There, he was able to befriend several doctors and nurses. He slowly finished off his degree, assisted mostly by the fact that many of the courses are now offered online and can be done year-round. He was able to add a few hours a week of volunteering in the children's ward. He helped doctors communicate with families that shared his mother tongue. He was well-liked and admired by the medical staff. They wrote him glowing recommendations that helped him achieve a spot in medical school. He is well on his way to becoming the doctor he's always wanted to be. He just didn't take the expected route. He created his own!

The moral of the story is, I didn't know *who* Abdoul was. I didn't know about his drive, perseverance, ingenuity, or ability to speak several languages. I saw him as a young man stuck in a job he didn't want, who would likely never get out. I am *so glad* I was wrong.

What else could we, as leaders, be wrong about? What other presumptions have we made about our staff and the people applying for our positions?

Being Overqualified

We also need to explore whether or not we have a bias regarding the education or experience we feel people should have entering a position. Working in HR has enabled me to meet thousands of people, to review their resumes and compare their experience and education to their requirements for the job. In some cases, the person may not initially appear to meet the requirements. However, the exciting part is to interview them anyway and find out what you can learn about who they are. Here is an example quite opposite to that of Abdoul. In this case, you are presented a resume under the name of Adel Smith. It outlines a very well-developed background, filled with years of experience in a field quite different from the one she is applying to. In fact, the job she is applying for is an entry position and doesn't require more than a high school education, yet she has a master's degree. What is your initial reaction to her resume? What questions come to mind? What assumptions are you making? *(Remember, no one but you knows what you are thinking, so feel free to be honest.)*

I am going to assume you are thinking about job fit and retention. After all, why would someone with a master's degree want an entry-level position, especially with the years of experience this person has? Are you concerned with them coming in and wanting to immediately move up in the organization, or worse yet, not even stay longer than six months? Is this just a "find a job while waiting for something better" kind of scenario? Will you toss the application aside based on your assumptions and concerns, or will you take the time to meet with her? If you did meet with Adel, you would soon discover she and her husband are now empty nesters. Both have held high-ranking positions, made a lot of money, saved for their daughter's education, and now they want to scale back. Despite the fact that she has previous managerial experience, she has *no* interest in moving up the corporate ladder. She wants to come to work, preferably in a part-time position, share her skills, and then travel with her husband. She doesn't want to be held down to a full-time job. She doesn't need benefits or a pension. She's just not ready to completely retire yet. So you hire her. She turns out to be an absolutely fantastic employee. She loves her job, does it well, and will happily share the part-time hours with younger staff members she knows need the hours. Aren't you glad you didn't throw that application aside?

I Hate My Job

Have you ever heard that from an employee? They are seemingly disgruntled and grumpy all of the time. They come to work in a bad mood and seem to pull everyone down with them. You don't know what to do or how to get them out of this "funk" they are in. You bring them in for a meeting and inevitably ask the question we all ask: "So what are your aspirations? Do you have some goals in the organization? Where do you see yourself in five years?"

What comes next is a forty-five-minute rant about how the organization has never done anything for them and they have watched as other, non-worthy people move up the corporate ladder and take positions they wanted. When you ask if they applied for the jobs or promotions, they yell back "NO, what's the point?" Are you smiling and picturing this exact scenario? The one where you wish you could just take the whole question back, and/or have your administrative assistant interrupt the meeting with an urgent message you need to immediately tend to?

In this case, clearly the person's answer to "what do you want to be?" would not have been the position they are currently in. Yet they seem unwilling to do anything about it. Do you find yourself going into solution-based problem solving, offering them ways they can get to where they want to be? That's okay, we all do it, but we need to remind ourselves to go back and look over the previous lessons learned and then think about taking another approach.

In Lesson 11, we learned about why some people don't trust the processes, and therefore may not even compete for positions they truly want.

In Lesson 14, we talked about making assumptions on how we can solve conflict and issues. We need to dig a little further into the root causes and needs this person has when it comes to employment, status, job role, etc.

In Lesson 15, we also acknowledged that we are not always listening for the meaning or context behind the comments. We are reacting as problem solvers and trying to potentially ease the tension of the situation, but if we listen, really listen, there is the potential to learn a lot.

In Lesson 18, we learned that a person's own background and experiences may be impacting the person's ability, or presumed ability, to move into a job they really want.

Taking a New Approach

What if, before jumping into problem-solving mode or escaping to a mystery emergency, you considered doing this? Rich Litvin has some fantastic YouTube videos on how you can better connect with people and truly find out how you can help them. One of the key phrases he uses when he meets with clients is, "How can I support you?" I really like this phrase. It doesn't allude to the fact that we have all the answers or can solve all the problems, but it does indicate we are open to listening and learning more.

Let's try it. The employee comes into your office. You need to discuss their attitude at work and how it is impacting other employees. However, instead of going with the assumption that their frustration lies primarily with the fact they have been unable to find their real purpose or have unmet goals, let's ask this instead: "Jerry, I have noticed that you seem really frustrated at work lately. I wanted to meet with you in hopes that I could better understand how I can support you as a manager. You are a valued employee, and I just want to try and understand more about what is behind your frustration." Now the next part is even harder—*say nothing else*. Stop talking. Just listen. If they don't reply initially, that's okay. Just sit in silence. You will be amazed with what happens.

Jerry will likely start to spew out some of the negative messaging about how they hate the organization and see themselves as a victim in an unfair, non-transparent process. But underneath this you will also hear their interests and needs. They want to be **respected for their experience** and want to be **challenged and feel worthy of their contributions**. You may even start to hear details that pertain to their individual and unique challenges. Maybe they tell you that they don't actually hate the job they are in, they just find the shift work really challenging and they have issues sleeping at night. Maybe it's the fact that working Monday to Friday, 8:00 a.m. to 4:00 p.m., doesn't allow them to get their son to needed medical appointments. Maybe they applied for and got this job years ago because it was the *responsible* thing to do and met family obligations, but it has never fulfilled their passion or interest. Maybe they really just want to quit but financially they can't afford to, and that reality is very stressful.

All of a sudden, your disgruntled employee is sharing what they *need* and *why*. The discussion has moved from *"what the organization is doing to make them miserable"* to more of one that allows you to discover *who* they are and what they need. All of a sudden, you have new potential ideas about how you can help. *But stop!* Don't go there. Remember, in Lesson 16 we discussed the need to help the person generate their own ideas, not solutions, and take the time to ensure we haven't missed anything. This is not a conversation that has to end in one meeting. Sometimes by scheduling a second meeting you are allowing the person time to reflect on what was discussed and consider new options. Often your role will be to simply listen and provide needed insight on certain topics. After all, this is their life and decisions. Given that the original context of the discussion was intended to make them aware of how they are impacting other people, this is a great time to introduce a behavioural assessment to them. Lesson 3 illustrated how doing a PI assessment, and then even comparing it to a teammate's helps people learn more about each other. Jerry's profile indicates they are that of a **Specialist**, so unlike me, they are uninterested in seeing the big picture or venturing outside the box. Under stress, they resort even more to their default behavioural traits of needing to see the world as black-and-white with structured rules and facts. They are skeptical of change and need to analyze suggested changes before making any decisions. They are in survival mode. You need to help them calm their nervous system, allowing them to move into the cognitive part of their brain and be open to other possibilities. This will take time. I have had such discussions. It's not easy; in fact, sometimes you will end up as exhausted as they sound, but it builds needed trust.

Generating New Ideas and Solutions

The ideas and solutions you work together to generate will vary and be unique to their needs.

1. In some cases, you may find ways to help accommodate them, no longer requiring them to work the night shifts. This will, in turn, assist with their sleep and their ability to reason and think, not to mention their mood.

2. You may even unearth the fact that they haven't applied for another job due to a fear of failure. In this case you will use strategies developed in Lesson 16 to assist them in feeling more confident in the interview.

3. Or it could be a case of their "hate" for the job being due to new processes and systems that are overwhelming, confusing, and feel beyond their capacity to learn. You may need to explore, giving them a different assignment within their own job while finding someone who can apply the coaching and training skills learned in Lesson 6.

Conversations such as this will help you as a leader as much as they will help the person in need. You will learn more about the issues and concerns facing your employees and why they potentially say the things they do. When you are completing performance appraisals, as described in Lesson 9, think about the goal section at the end of the assessment. "What are your goals and action plans for the next year?" Try and guard yourself against wanting to assess the worth of their goal. Instead, listen to what is behind it. Remember how insidious social expectations and biases are and how they may impact both your and the employee's view of what they can accomplish and which goals are suitable.

LESSON 20

Silos Need to Be Eradicated

Can Organizations Really Change?

Let's begin by having you rate your organization's progress on a score-card. How do you feel your leaders are doing when it comes to *effectively leading others?*

In answering, consider the following:

- Try not to fall victim to the rater biases learned in Lesson 9. Although it is tempting to picture only a couple of recent scenarios in your head, and/or the behaviour of one particular leader, try to rate the organization as a whole. If one leader does stand out to you, compare this name to your list in Lesson 4. Are these behaviours you want to emulate or ones you want to avoid?

- After each question, think about how processes could be potentially enhanced using strategies introduced in this book.

Rating Your Organization's Leadership Techniques

1. During meetings do you, as leaders, listen to each other and allow others to share ideas?

    a. Yes
    b. No

Are there ways this process could be enhanced?

2. Is there a tendency for one or more persons to dominate conversation, interrupt, and talk over others in the meetings? Is this behaviour permitted?

    a. Yes
    b. No

Are there ways this process could be enhanced?

3. When setting priorities, do leaders take into consideration the impact it will have on other units, branches, and people within your organization? *(For example, if my project becomes a priority, this may impact your goals and staffing.)*

    a. Yes
    b. No

Are there ways this process could be enhanced?

4. When there is a conflict in the workplace, do you, as leaders, attempt to resolve it by transferring people and/or dealing with surface issues, or do you attempt to resolve the issue and rebuild relationships?

    a. Surface issues
    b. Rebuild relationships

Are there ways this process could be enhanced?

5. Have your leaders readjusted their leadership style to suit a virtual workforce?

   a. Are leaders checking in with employees to determine how the process has been for them?

   b. Are leaders holding themselves accountable for issues they may have played a part in (i.e., missed emails, micromanaging, different game with the same rules)?

Are there ways this process could be enhanced?

6. After reading Lessons 17, 18, and 19, do you feel your organization is making a concerted effort to ensure you have an equitable and inclusive workplace?

   a. Yes

   b. No

Can you think of examples?
Are there ways these processes could be enhanced?

7. How does your organization ensure people are feeling valued and heard?

8. What is your organization's retention rate overall?

   a. Can this data be broken down to address specific retention rate concerns?

9. Do you know why people choose to leave the organization? If so, what are the common reasons?

10. After reading this book, are their key strategies you would like to introduce to your organization? If so, which ones and why?

Where to Go from Here

You may be wondering, *Where do we go from here?* You might be ready to throw down this book again. You may be looking over your responses and feeling frustrated. Try not to focus on one negative answer or one leader you are frustrated with. It's very easy to go into the mindset that *this will never work. They are never going to change,* and you are right. Not everyone in the organization is willing or able to do the work necessary to alter their conduct, listen more effectively, consider other people's needs and interests, resolve conflict by getting to the root of the issue, and/or refrain from immediately jumping to solution-based problem solving. These are the leaders that tell us "oh, I read that leadership book, I took that course," but do nothing to grow and evolve in their leadership. That's okay. That's about them, not about you. It doesn't mean we all have to give up. I believe that if enough people in an organization want to lead more effectively and get help learning the skills, then the change will start to happen organically. Eventually others will have to join the parade or allow for a changing of the guard. The most important element is that you are showing an interest in learning about *who* you are leading, what you need to do to build trust, and how to help employees feel heard and valued in your organization. If you work on these skills, then you will start to ensure ideas are shared, priorities are set with everyone in mind, and communication is enhanced. In his book *Silos, Politics, and Turf Wars,* Patrick Lencioni tells us that "Silos within organizations evolve from barriers that exist between departments, causing people who are supposed to be on the same team to work against each other. If there is a place where the blame for silos and politics belongs, it is at the top of an organization. Every departmental silo in a company can ultimately be traced back to the leaders of those departments who have failed to understand the interdependencies that must exist among the executive team, or who have failed to make those interdependencies clear to the people deeper in their own departments" (175–177).

We all need to understand *who* we are, how we contribute to our team and our organization. We need to learn how to relate our own strengths and behaviours to the potential contributions we can offer. We also need to learn to appreciate the strengths that others contribute. We need to learn to be open to the possibility that those different from ourselves actually enhance our life.

Building Unity and Understanding

I believe that training and team-building exercises, designed with a purpose, can assist organizations and their personnel to build needed unity, trust, and understanding. In addition to using PI assessments, trust-building exercises, and MI quizzes, I have also used an exercise entitled the "leadership compass" to further break down silos and enhance the appreciation we have for others. It was developed from Indigenous teachings of the medicine wheel or the "Four-Fold Way." The four leadership directions are described as warrior (north), healer (south), teacher (west), and visionary (east). Each plays a key role in the success of an organization (LEADright).[10]

THE PERSONALITY COMPASS

Everyone has some characteristics from each of the four directions, but one will capture the essence of your personality more accurately than the others. That is your primary direction.

No one direction is better than another, they're all just different.

NORTH
Natural leader;
Goal-oriented; Fast-paced;
Task-oriented; Assertive;
Decisive; Confident;
Determined; Competitive;
Independant

WEST
Natural risk taker;
Idea-centered; Creative;
Innovative; Flexible;
Visionary; Spontaneous;
Enthusiastic; Free-spirited;
Energetic

EAST
Natural planner;
Quality-centered;
Analytical; Organized;
Logical; Focused; Exact;
Perfectionist; Industrious;
Structured

SOUTH
Natural team player;
Process-centered;
Slow-paced; Good listener;
Non-confrontational;
Sensitive; Patient;
Understanding; Generous;
Helpful

This is a very effective exercise to encourage groups to learn to appreciate the skills each member brings. It can be done in a physical classroom or a virtual one. It starts by asking people to answer a series of questions

---

10   The following graphic and exercise can be accessed as a PDF on my website- www.inspiringorganizationalgrowth.ca.

about how they like to make decisions and work with others (similar to ones you answered in Lesson 7). Based on their responses, they are identified as being primarily north, south, east, or west. Now the fun begins. Participants are then asked to divide themselves up into groups according to their compass assignment. The small groups then answer another set of questions:

1. What do you feel are your greatest strengths?
2. What are your weaknesses?
3. What other groups do you like to work with most?
4. What other groups do you like to work with *least*? Why?
5. What do you appreciate about each of the other groups?

The groups then form a large compass formation. In a classroom setting, "north" participants stand together at the top of the circle, "west" to the right, "east" to the left, and "south" to the base of the circle. This can be adjusted to suit your virtual platform as well. A group spokesperson is asked to read their responses out loud (usually "north" participants will volunteer to go first). Question 5, in particular, brings out a lot of the learning. It highlights that despite our differences, we need each other's skills and strengths to supplement our own "weaknesses," or as PI assessments term it, "cautionary behaviours." Participants realize that although they do need the "warriors" who will take charge, make decisions, and accept risk, they also need the other groups: the "healers" who help to ensure everyone's needs are heard and met, the "teachers" who take the time to examine all the issues and details before a decision is made, and the "visionaries" who introduce new ideas and the possibility of innovative thinking. Together they develop an appreciation for the work each group does and exemplify the need to break down silos.

Breaking Down Silos

Using strategies such as these can enable you, as a leader, to inspire organizational change. Developing respect and understanding for what each of your employees can bring to the table, and then celebrating those unique differences, can be transformational to an organization. I have personally witnessed how lifelong silos have started to crumble when leaders took the time to learn more about each other. People I originally would have labelled as difficult, argumentative, and stubborn evolved into people I knew I could rely on and who would give me an honest opinion and insight. I realized that their loyalty to their team, their need for detail, and their discomfort with risk made them an extremely valuable member. Blending our abilities enabled us to build connections between our teams and work together to succeed and find viable solutions. Having different learning styles, needs, interests, and approaches enhances the experience. We just had to ensure we left our egos at the door and stayed curious.

PUTTING THE LESSONS TO WORK

Moving Forward

W e have covered a lot of material in this book, and I have hopefully provided you with a lot to think about. To give you a starting point, I have designed a reference list you can use to potentially enhance your own leadership capacity and growth mindset. It covers many of the elements we have discussed in this book and gives you a process to use. Recognizing that each of you have different learning styles and behaviour preferences, I have made the list inclusive enough that you can follow it step by step or select only elements that appeal to you. In her book *Mindset, the New Psychology of Success,* Carol S. Dweck, PhD, effectively describes the process leaders need to use. "Those with a growing mindset kept on learning. When you enter the world of growth-mindset leaders, everything changes. It brightens, it expands, it fills with energy, with possibility. As a growth-minded leader, they start with the belief in human potential and development—both their own and other people's" (125).

Strapping on Your *New* Leadership Skates

Let's start from the beginning. You have just strapped on your new leadership "skates"—so let's get ready for the real game. Let's review what we have learned and how it can be used to inspire your own growth and that of your team.[11]

Inspiring Organizational Growth Checklist

Part 1—It All Starts with You

- Do your own Predictive Index (PI) assessment (**Lesson 3**)
- Review the results with a trained PI practitioner
- Review the leadership styles (**Lesson 4**)
- Review your "Leaders in Your Life and How They Lead" chart (**Lesson 4**) to enhance your understanding of who you want to emulate in your own leadership
- Review the recommended readings in the "Works Cited" list at the end of the book. Are there areas you would like to learn more about, expand your skills in, and challenge yourself to re-examine?
- Complete your own Multiple Intelligence (MI) quiz to discover how you learn (**Lesson 6**)
- Complete the quiz "Who Do You Like to Work With?" (**Lesson 7**)
- Review the listening modes (**Lesson 14**)

Part 2—Who Are You Leading?

- Share your MI quiz with your staff/team/unit (**Lesson 6**)
- Share your PI assessment with them (**Lesson 3**)
- Encourage members of your team to do their MI and PI assessments (**Lessons 3 and 6**)
- Utilize the information gained to create coaching and training strategies (**Lesson 6**)
- Apply job assessment information from the PIs to create job descriptions/postings for new hires (**Lesson 7**)
- Review the quiz "Who Do You Like to Work With?" to ensure you are looking for the ideal job candidate—not *your* ideal candidate (**Lesson 7**)

---

11   This checklist can also be found on my website: www.inspiringorganizationalgrowth.ca. I have also created a Leadership Goal Planner that works with the checklist, to encourage leaders to hold themselves accountable and set viable action plans.

Part 3—Developing Trust, Removing Triggers, and Building Teams

- Review how to use the PI to provide feedback to employees who are unsuccessful in a position **(Lesson 8)**
- Re-read your "labelling chart" to capture the impact labels have on others **(Lesson 5)**
- Implement a "rules of engagement" exercise into your group meetings **(Lesson 10)**
- Use information from PI assessments to help team members better understand each other **(Lesson 12)**
- Get to the root cause, issue, needs, and interests of people engaged in conflict **(Lesson 14)**
- Complete the "triggers activity/exercise" with your team **(Lesson 10)**
- Challenge yourself to listen and not jump into problem solving/solution-based role **(Lessons 12 to 14)**

Part 4—Putting Lessons Learned into Practice

- Review your performance evaluations and rating processes **(Lesson 9)**
- Review rater biases to ensure objectivity when completing performance reviews **(Lesson 9)**
- Use MI, PI, and job assessments to help provide feedback for interviews **(Lesson 16)**
- Create a team PI assessment chart **(Lesson 12)**
- Develop virtual meeting strategies **(Lesson 13)**
- Schedule check-ins with your employees **(Lesson 13)**

Part 5—Inspiring Organizational Growth

- Ensure remote team members feeling included and heard **(Lesson 13)**
- Review process that needs to change to suit a virtual setting **(Lesson 13)**
- Consider the unique and diverse aspects of your employees when asking about goal setting **(Lesson 19)**

- Create ways to hear from those your decisions impact (internal and external surveys, community feedback sessions, small working groups, etc.) **(Lesson 17)**
- Invite members of your organization to participate in reviewing processes/policies/practices that impact them **(Lesson 18)**
- Review the use of free or low-paying internships, grant positions, volunteer and co-op positions—can they be improved? **(Lesson 18)**
- Review list of diversity questions—do you have the answers? **(Lesson 17)**
- Try exercises like the "leadership compass" to further break down silos **(Lesson 20)**
- Utilize leadership and organizational training opportunities as a way of not only developing the "hard skills" but also the "soft skills" needed to create understanding, inclusive workplaces, and enhanced relationships **(Lesson 20)**

Leadership Goal Planner

I have designed a Leadership Goal Planner for you to utilize in conjunction with the Growth Checklist. Its purpose is to help you to organize your thoughts, set new goals and hold yourself accountable to follow through on action plans you set. It will challenge you to examine why things are occurring, and what you need to do to improve them. Leadership is a journey, and this goal planner will help you develop a path forward.

If you are interested in the planner, it can be found on my author's page on my website: www.inspiringorganizationalgrowth.ca.

Receiving Your Feedback and Insight

I would love to hear from you and learn what you have taken from the book. What are your personal leadership experiences and challenges? Have you been able to implement any of the ideas generated in this book? Did they work? I hope to hear from leaders like you and encourage you to share your insight and ideas with others. Join in the conversation with other inspiring leaders by visiting my author's page on my website: www.inspiringorganizationalgrowth.ca

LEARNING BEYOND THE BOOK

Being an Outsider Helps

"My goal in life is to try new things. It helps you
change your perspective and keep learning."

—Robin Williams

It was this notion that led me to taking the initial step in creating my business focused on inspiring organizational growth. It has been developed to help leaders like you further enhance their skills, apply new ones, and receive one-on-one coaching when needed. My experience as a mediator, HR professional, and interview coach has enabled me to develop resources, tools, courses, and services that organizations can utilize to help resolve issues and ensure a healthy and inclusive workplace. I also realized that, as leaders, sometimes we get stuck and need some guidance or "mid-game" coaching to help us through the tough parts of the game. When the team isn't gelling well together and there is inner conflict or disgruntled members, we may need someone from the outside to come in, instill trust, and listen to what the underlying concerns are. Even though we mean well as leaders, we are often too invested or simply unable to provide the needed guidance to our team. We learned in Lesson 4 that there are many different leadership styles and that we can't be all things to all people. We need to identify our strengths but also acknowledge areas where we might need to call up another player or coach to teach or assist with a play or developing a new game plan.

Watching from the Bleachers

Sometimes you need to bring someone else in to help the team instead of just observing the game from the bleachers. In my experience as an HR professional, I always needed to ensure I was viewed as being objective and impartial. This meant I couldn't interfere in the game, even when I knew "players" needed help. For example, even though I had the skills and knowledge to help internal members with their interview prep, I couldn't be seen as favouring one person more than another. I had to try and ensure that any advice I gave one person was equal to that I provided another.

I am sure you have had similar experiences. After reading this book, the next time you are sitting in meeting, you will be much more aware of why issues are happening (people aren't hearing each other, people are jumping to solution-based discussions, people's needs and learning styles are not being met). Sometimes you will be able to intervene and offer new strategies, but in other cases, it may not be your place to do so. After all, they are your coworkers and bosses. Who are you to speak up and suggest how they can potentially improve communications and processes? When conflict does arise, sometimes you won't be best person to address it.

In other instances, when you do try to help, people might become skeptical. They see you as part of "them, the administration" and don't believe you can be impartial. They are fearful to share too much of themselves; therefore, despite your best efforts, the conversations often remain "surface level" and doesn't reveal the deeper issues and concerns. Without this information, the real issues are never revealed or addressed. I suspect the same is true in all organizations. That's why I have also created my business, Inspiring Organizational Growth. Sometimes you need to bring in someone from the outside who can "watch from the bleachers" to make observations and provide guidance. If you think I can help you and your organization, please contact me. My goal is to support leaders and their teams, enabling them to build trust and engage in needed conversations.

Creating the Time to Listen

In her *Dare to Lead Podcast,* Brené Brown discusses with Charles Feltman his book *The Thin Book of Trust,* wherein he explains the importance of creating trust. He explains that when someone chooses to trust you, they are choosing to risk making something they value vulnerable to another person's actions. Just think about how powerful it is to have someone trust you. It also puts into greater perspective *why* people may not always be willing or able to fully share something vulnerable with you. At times, the most respectful thing you can do, as their leader, is to acknowledge the need to provide them with someone else to talk to, someone who is trained to listen with an open heart and who will ask "How can I support you?"

This is where my role as a skilled consultant allows me to truly make a difference in organizations. As an outsider, I can offer my services free of any internal obligations or apparent biases. I can come into your organization, listen to your needs, dig deep to uncover causation, work to build needed trust, and then design services to meet your needs. I can coach, train, speak, facilitate conversations, mediate issues, and promote growth.

Mediating Conflict

As we discussed in Lesson 14, conflict in the workplace is inevitable. Let me help you learn more about your organization and the issues that may be below the surface. Let me help to rebuild relationships between people that have been at odds for years. If there is one thing I have learned, it's that issues *never* go away until they are finally truly addressed. Corporate memory is not just about the skills and knowledge that we carry with us; it is also about the people that you feel crossed you, did you an injustice, weren't held accountable, and didn't validate your feelings.

The same way we helped Jan and Darryl work through some of their underlying needs and gain a better understanding of each other, I think there is a huge need to do the same in your workplaces. Think back to some of your own conflicts you have had with coworkers. Were they isolated events, or did they stem from deeper underlying issues about who the people involved are, how they operate, what they value, and how they react to having differing opinions? Are there people who, to this day, you have never really been able to get past issues with? Would it have helped if you had been offered an outsider "listener" of sorts, someone who came in, heard from both of you, helped to get to the root of the issues and then helped *you* generate potential solutions and ideas? How many years of further discourse and mistrust could this have helped to prevent?

Introducing New Tools

One of my additional goals is to help leaders learn more about the people they are leading. We have discussed how getting to know your employees will guide you in learning how to select, mentor, train, empower, and retain them. As a trained PI practitioner, I want to help introduce this tool to more leaders and organizations. So many elements of what I do and have learned have been enhanced by using this behavioural tool. Regardless of whether you are leading a small business or a huge profit-making organization, you can benefit from learning more about your people than is written on a resume, biography, or performance evaluation. I want to demonstrate to leaders how this valuable information can be helpful in all stages of employment.

Developing Healthy Teams

I also offer support to your leaders and their teams. I recognize many of your staff are already skilled and experienced in many aspects of leadership. They have taken dozens of courses, read many of the books I have quoted in my book, and together have decades, if not centuries, of experience. That's perfect. What I really do is just be a *fly on the wall*. I sit in your meetings and watch as all of you interact. I sit in your boardrooms (virtual or physical), in your planning sessions, on the job site, and just listen and observe. Just as the mentoring hockey coach does from the stands, I recognize the need for observation and conversation. I will use strategies to learn more about each of your leaders and what makes them tick. I am willing to take the time to listen and build trust. I will invite people to complete their PIs, and together we will create a safe space to share what we have learned. This process can be a lot of fun and incredibly enlightening to those involved. It isn't punitive or linked to some kind of investigation aimed at pointing fingers and finding blame. Instead, it is an exercise in learning more about each other. Just as we found in Lessons 12 and 13, doing small exercises—such as "What are things that help you learn, what are things that impact your learning?"—can help a team gel more. And just as we learned in Lessons 10 and 11, there will also be a need to help teammates learn how they impact each other, and determine each person's needs and concerns. Together, with you as leaders, we can generate a safe space to increase needed dialogue and generate connection.

Training and Facilitation

As a trained adult facilitator who has designed and delivered many leadership, coaching, and interest based courses, I understand the value in effective training. Whether it is an exercise in listening, orally communicating, delivering feedback, or learning how we impact one another, we need to be able to relate it back to what the session goals are. We need to leave the course or training feeling more equipped and skilled than when we came. We need to be able to ask the tough questions and demand proof that the skills being presented will work. I have spent years developing and facilitating leadership-training courses with just this purpose in mind. I won't sugar-coat the content, and if my methods can be challenged and enhanced, all the better. Every time I write a syllabus it is slightly different from the last. I will make it suit learners' needs. Even if the title of the course is the same, I will encompass new ideas, new learning, and suggestions from past learners. I want to ensure that my content is meeting the needs of all my learners and their multiple learning styles and interests. Just as we discussed in Lesson 2, I want to ensure this isn't just another #$!% leadership course. I want to work with organizations to discover what they need and how we can address those outcomes.

Consulting with Leaders

After reading this book, you may feel a need to re-examine existing policies, practices, and processes. It may also result in the need to have some candid and honest discussions about how you are hiring and developing your employees. You may have now recognized that, as an organization, your forms and processes may not be as inclusive as they need to be. It may be that some of your coaches and supervisors are stuck and seemingly unwilling to change. It all takes time and a willingness to do the deep organizational dive. Let me help you with that. I can let you focus on your job while I dissect who you are as an organization and help you grow. I also want to help you do some of the preliminary work to build needed consultation groups and processes, built from trust and open dialogue.

One-to-One Leadership Coaching

Organizations who invest in providing their leaders and supervisors with a one-on-one coach have discovered it has a very healthy return on investment. Leaders who are willing to work with a coach enhance not only their own experiences and skills but also the skills and talents of those they lead. My leadership coaching involves working with leaders in virtual sessions. We focus on goals and issues they wish to address, explore their leadership style and its impact, develop tools and strategies they wish to try, and then meet again to discuss what is working, what isn't, and how we can apply other tools and learning to "deal with the real-life workplace issues they are facing." I refer to this as "coaching with you on the bench". Every great hockey team has a co-coaching system. We all need someone to bounce ideas off, discuss strategy, and ask for feedback. I will "sit on the bench" with you and help you work your way through the season, allowing you to build a trusting and engaged team, one that scores goals, wins games, increases productivity and profits.

Let Me Help You (Virtual or In-Person)

This is the work I absolutely *love* doing. It has taken me 25 years of experience, training, and skill development to get to where I am. As a consultant, mediator, trainer, and coach I am professionally equipped to help you with your organization and personal leadership development. I think it is key that we, as leaders, work together to decipher and overcome the challenges our positions present. Let me help you work through the various situations, scenarios, conflicts, and issues that are arising and affecting your workplace. We can work together to learn more about your leadership styles, the behaviours and traits of those you lead, and utilize the skills and tools mentioned in this book to get to the root of the issues and find viable solutions.

If you think I could be of any further assistance to you or your organization, please reach out to me at www.inspiringorganizationalgrowth.ca

Being given the opportunity to lead and mentor others is a true honour. We owe it to those we lead to do the best job we can and to ask for help when we need it. Learning more about who you are and the people you lead will help you to truly inspire, build trust, and mentor those around you. Thank you for taking the time and investing the energy into reading this book. I hope that you take these elements, lessons, and ideas and now institute them into your own leadership journey.

Inspiring Organizational Growth

Recommended Readings
and Works Cited

Bartleby. "Remote Workers Work Longer, Not More Efficiently." *The Economist*, The Economist Newspaper Limited, 12 June 2021, www.economist.com. Accessed 7 November 2021.

Bethea, Aiko. "Creating Transformative Cultures—Brené Brown." *Brené Brown*, 8 February 2021, https://brenebrown.com/podcast/brene-with-aiko-bethea-on-creating-transformative-cultures/. Accessed 11 February 2022.

Bethea, Aiko. "An Open Letter to Corporate America, Philanthropy, Academia, etc.: What Now?" *Aiko Bethea*, 1 June 2020, https://aikobethea.medium.com/an-open-letter-to-corporate-america-philanthropy-academia-etc-what-now-8b2d3a310f22. Accessed 11 February 2022.

"Brené with Charles Feltman on Trust: Building, Maintaining, and Restoring It." *Brené Brown*, 4 October 2021, https://brenebrown.com/podcast/trust-building-maintaining-and-restoring-it/. Accessed 25 January 2022.

Brown, Brené. *Braving the Wilderness*. New York, Random House, 2017.

Brown, Brené. *Dare to Lead*. New York, Random House, 2018.

Brown, Jeff. *Read to Lead*. Podcast. 2016. *Read to Lead Podcast*, Brown Knows Media LLC, readtolead.com. Accessed 08 October 2021.

Bungay Stanier, Micheal. *The Coaching Habit—Say Less, Ask More & Change the Way You Lead Forever*. Audiobook, 2016.

Burley, Jodi-Ann. "The myth of bringing your full, authentic self to work." *ted.com*, TEDxSeattle, www.ted.com/talks/jodi_ann_burley_the_myth_of_bringing_your_full_authentic_self_to_work. Accessed 24 October 2021.

Clemens, David. "Conflict management training: A frequently missed opportunity." *Rapid Learning Institute*, 20 October 2021, https://rapidlearninginstitute.com/blog/conflict-management-training-a-frequently-missed-opportunity/. Accessed 24 January 2022.

Clifton, Don, et al. *First, Break All the Rules*. First ed., New York, Gallup Press, 2016.

"The Daily—After five years of increases, police-reported crime in Canada was down in 2020, but incidents of hate crime increased sharply." *Statistique Canada*, 27 July 2021, https://www150.statcan.gc.ca/n1/daily-quotidien/210727/dq210727a-eng.htm. Accessed 24 January 2022.

"The Daily—Labour Force Survey, December 2021." *Statistique Canada*, 7 January 2022, https://www150.statcan.gc.ca/n1/daily-quotidien/220107/dq220107a-eng.htm. Accessed 25 January 2022.

Deer, K. "Why it's difficult to put a number on how many children died at residential schools." *CBC*, 29 September 2021, https://www.cbc.ca/news/indigenous/residential-school-children-deaths-numbers-1.6182456. Accessed 24 January 2022.

Dweck, Carole S. *Mindset-The New Psychology of Success*. New York, Ballantine Books, 2008.

Feltman, Charles. *The Thin Book of Trust: An Essential Primer for Building Trust at Work*. Thin Book Publishing Inc, 2009. Accessed 31 October 2021.

Friday, Rob. *Talent Optimizer*. RobFriday.com, 2019.

Fuller, Pamela, et al. *The Leader's Guide to Unconscious Bias*. New York, Franklin Covey Co, 2020.

Gallup. *Strengths Based Leadership*. New York, Gallup Press, 2008.

Goleman, Daniel. *Emotional Intelligence*. New York, Bantam Books, 1995.

Hitchcock, Ken. "Ken Hitchcock about coaching millenials." *Coach Kirill*, 23 January 2019, https://youtu.be/lmsvDHeXWmE. Accessed 25 October 2021.

Holiday, Ryan. *Ego Is the Enemy*. New York, Portfolio/Penguin, 2016.

Indeed Editor Team. "Top 12 Common Management Challenges." *Indeed*, Indeed, 9 June 2021, ca.indeed.com. Accessed 8 August 2021.

Indigenous Corporate Training Inc. "First Nation Talk Stick Protocol." *ictinc.ca*, Blue Pixel Design, 2021, www.ictinc.ca. Accessed 30 October 2021.

"Just the Facts—Poverty in Canada." *Canada Without Poverty*, 2022, https://cwp-csp.ca/poverty/just-the-facts/. Accessed 25 January 2022.

Lahey, David. *From Hire to Inspire: How to Become the Best Boss*. Toronto, ECW press, 2020.

Lahey, David. *Predicting Success*. New Jersey, John Wiley and Sons Inc, 2015.

LEADright. "We Coach and Train Leaders and Learners For Excellence." *leadrighttoday*, leadrighttoday.com.

Lencioni, Patrick. *The Five Dysfunctions of a Team*. San Francisco, Jossey-Bass, 2002.

Lencioni, Patrick. *Silos, Politics, and Turf Wars*. San Francisco, Jossey-Bass, 2006.

Liker, Jeffrey K., and Gary L. Convis. *The Toyota Way to Lean Leadership*. First ed., New York, McGraw-Hill, 2012.

Litvin, Rich. "How to Become a Master Coach." *YouTube*, Evercoach by Mindvalley, 22 August 2019, youtu.be/kb71A5gyJ2M. Accessed 21 June 2021.

Martinuzzi, Bruna. "7 Common Leadership Styles and How to Find Yours." *American Express*, 21 July 202, https://www.americanexpress.com/en-us/business/trends-and-insights/articles/the-7-most-common-leadership-styles-and-how-to-find-your-own. Accessed 22 August 2021.

Maxwell, John C. *Failing Forward*. Nashville, Thomas Nelson, 2000.

McKee, Annie, et al. *Becoming a Resonant Leader*. Boston, Harvard Business Press, 2008.

Melfi, Theodore, director. *Hidden Figures*. 20th Century Fox, 2016.

"Mental Illness and Addiction: Facts and Statistics." CAMH, 2022, https://www.camh.ca/en/driving-change/the-crisis-is-real/mental-health-statistics. Accessed 24 January 2022.

Noble, Cinnie. *Conflict Management Coaching—The Cinergy Model*. Canada, CINERGY Coaching, 2012.

Noble, Cinnie. *Conflict Mastery—Questions to Guide You*. Canada, CINERGY Coaching, 2014.

OxfordLanguages. "Microaggressions." Oxford Languages, Oxford University Press, 2021, www.languages.oup.com. Accessed 31 October 2021.

Rana, Uday. "For many newcomers, 'Canadian experience' remains a barrier to meaningful employment." The Globe and Mail, 18 December 2021, https://www.theglobeandmail.com/canada/article-for-many-newcomers-canadian-experience-remains-a-barrier-to-meaningful/. Accessed 18 January 2022.

Rose, Todd. *The End of Average*. Toronto, Harper Collins, 2016.

Soar Learning. "Multiple Intelligence Quiz." Soarlearning, SOAR, soar-learning.com. Accessed 22 July 2021.

Statistics Canada. "Working from Home: Productivity and Preferences." StatCan COVID-19, Stats Can, 01 April 2021, www.150.statscan.gc.ca. Accessed 6 November 2021.

TG Innerselves. "TG Innerselves." Ghost Tigress, 2012, tginnerselves.com. Accessed 19 May 2021.

"TransPULSECanada." Trans PULSE Canada—Home, 26 August 2021, https://transpulsecanada.ca/. Accessed 18 January 2022.

Vengoechea, Ximena. *Reclaiming The Lost Art of True Connection—Listen Like You Mean It.* First ed., New York, Portfolio/Penguin, 2021.

Vitale, Jim. "Hockey Scout: 5 Things They Always Look For." Vital Hockey Skills, Inview Marketing, 30 May 2021, www.vitalhockeyskills.com. Accessed 11 December 2021.

ABOUT THE AUTHOR

Carrie-Lynn Hotson holds a Bachelor of Arts in Law and Psychology, Certified Human Resources Leader accreditation (CHRL) and is a graduate of Interest-Based Mediation training. She has 25 years of experience as a coach, facilitator, and leader, including seven years as a senior human resources manager with extensive experience addressing workplace issues and organizational challenges.

Hotson's expertise in interviewing, onboarding, and training informed her interview coaching business, jobinterviewcoach.ca. What Hotson gleaned from meeting candidates, learning about their skills and abilities, and gaining insight into why they are seeking to leave their current employment has been integrated into her book, *Knowing Who You Lead*. These key lessons will help current and future leaders empower, engage, and retain employees. Hotson has now expanded her services to include the coaching and mentoring of leaders in her second business inspiringorganizationalgrowth.ca.

Hotson lives in Sudbury, Ontario, on a 140-acre farm with her husband, daughter, two horses, beef cattle, and two dogs. She also has three grown sons, a fabulous daughter-in-law and three wonderful grandchildren.